Millionaire Mentality

BY DEXTER YAGER

With Doug Wead

Internet Services Corporation
Charlotte, N.C.

DEDICATED TO:

Leonard E. Yager, Sr.
Sam Simpkins
Stan Joslyn
Ken Reymore
Rich De Vos and Jay Van Andel,
whose principles taught me how
to be an achiever.
Gertrude Yager
John Dexter
Leon Dexter
Grandma Dexter, who taught
me to never lose my sense
of humor.
Greta Washer
Harry Rossiter, who taught
me to keep dreaming.

TABLE OF CONTENTS

Chapter Five:

THINKING STRAIGHT!........................59

Chapter Six:

SQUEEZE, SQUEEZE, SQUEEZE! 75

Chapter Seven:

A-SHOPPING WE WILL GO! 99

Chapter Eight:

INVESTMENTS 113

INTRODUCTION

Twenty years ago, I was a young man with a growing family, struggling to make ends meet. While my wages were considered good and there appeared to be security working for a large corporation, it became apparent that the needs of my family would soon outstrip the income. In addition, the prejudice against those with limited formal education made my chances for climbing the corporate ladder very slim. The idea of spending the next 35 to 40 years of my life stuck in the same job with little or no chance of advancement held no appeal. I was determined to do something about my situation.

Upon evaluating my goals and desires for life, I realized that for me to feel fulfilled, it would be necessary to help other people. This was not an easy decision. I had no college degree to provide credibility. Speaking was difficult because of a severe stutter. There was no money. What I did have was a goal. I began immediately to develop a plan to attain my desire.

The first step in the plan was to achieve the financial independence that would allow me to fulfill my aim. Though I didn't realize it at the time, the lessons learned in this step were to become the basis for the accomplishment of my life's work.

Most of us go through life believing that it is the rich who are most likely to be tempted by "the love of money." Yet, when we evaluate the situation, we find that those in financial need are the ones who must constantly spend time that could otherwise be used creatively, worrying about funds to pay bills and provide the basics of life. It is the poor who are most likely to go through life without achieving their potential because of preoccupation with money—or the lack of it.

Studying those who have achieved financial security, it becomes obvious that there are two elements necessary to acquiring that status—sufficient wealth to meet monetary needs, and the skill to manage the funds available. The possession of wealth is not in itself sufficient to provide financial security. Many great fortunes have been squandered through mismanagement. Thus the development of money management skills becomes paramount.

Unless you have been born to wealth, there are only two ways to deal with cash flow needs: lower your economic wants, or increase the income available. Financial need is no respecter of persons. It can affect the educated and the ignorant, the young or the old, the great and the common. Sometimes, even those who may be judged wealthy overextend their resources. A recently-discovered letter shows that even the President of the United States can find himself in a cash flow bind. Dated November 27, 1803, the note addressed to one Craven Payton requested a delay in the payment of a bill due or its conversion to installment payments. The signature was T.H. Jefferson, and the envelope bore the return address: T. Jefferson, President, U.S.

Applying the lessons learned by others to my own situation, financial independence was very shortly within my grasp, and, with it, the freedom to pursue my dream of helping others to achieve their potential in life. I determined that the best way to help others was to teach them how to be financially free to strive for their goals. Success for me was best defined as "the progressive realization of a worthwhile goal or dream."

During the past twenty years, I have been able to help thousands of people develop a plan for achieving financial security to allow them to pursue their goals. The purpose of this book is to acquaint you with the principles for achieving sufficient cash flow and the money management skills necessary to be financially independent.

Chapter One

WHERE DO I GO FROM HERE?

In the Broadway musical South Pacific, one of the lines from the song, "Happy Talk," puts it succinctly, "You gotta have a dream. If you don't have a dream, how you gonna have a dream come true?" Ask yourself: Why do I want to acquire wealth? For most of us, mere acquisition is not sufficient reason to discipline ourselves to do what is necessary. A goal, or dream, is the carrot we use to develop the disciplines for acquiring wealth and to manage what is accumulated.

One of the largest bank failures in United States history took place in the early 1980's. Penn Square Bank of Oklahoma was placed in receivership after federal bank examiners found the company had extended unsound loans to several energy companies.

At the same time, Wall Street began to take notice of another Oklahoma bank, Liberty National, which had seen its net income grow a steady 15% per year since 1972 as it became the second largest bank in Oklahoma.

The growth of Liberty National took place under the leadership of its chairman, Bill McLean. McLean received his experience in the banking centers of Houston and San Francisco, but he attributes much of Liberty's steady performance to the management principle of goal-setting, which he learned from his biblical studies. He is particularly fond of the parable of the talents found in Matthew 25:14-30. "To every one who has will more be given, and he will have abundance; but from him who has not, even what he has will be taken away."

Put it on Paper

Begin with a sheet of paper and write across the top: "If money were no object." Then list your answers to the questions: Who would I help? What kind of car would I drive? What would I provide my wife, my family? Where would I travel? What would I do with my time if I were financially free? In other words, if you had the time and financial resources, what would you do with your life?

It is essential that this process be done on paper! There is a psychological commitment that occurs when we put something in writing. As long as we don't write down a goal or desire, we can tell ourselves, "Well, I didn't want that anyway." However, once we've put our dream in writing, we can't fool ourselves anymore.

Putting our goals in writing does something in addition to keeping us from fooling ourselves. Once we have committed our conscious mind to the existence of a purpose by putting it in writing, we also release the relentless powers of our subconscious to turn its efforts toward reaching the goal.

How Much Will I Need?

The next step is to select one of your goals and convert that dream into the specific amount of money necessary to attain it. Even though you have several goals, it is necessary to establish priorities. Singleness of purpose is essential to the accomplishment of an aim. As one destination comes into reach, a new target is set. Remember the definition of success: "The progressive realization of a worthwhile goal or dream." After succeeding with one goal, you'll be able to handle more at a time. I keep a dozen or more major goals going at once.

It is not necessary that you select a goal that you think you can reach at the time you select it. If you will follow the pattern outlined in this book, you will learn to believe in your plan for reaching your dreams.

When Do I Want It?

After selecting a target and determining the specific amount of money necessary to meet that objective, the third step is to assign a specific date by which you intend to acquire the money. There is a natural reluctance to assign a specific time to any goal. "What if I don't meet the date?" That old nemesis, "fear of failure," raises its ugly head. So what? Shrug it off. If you don't meet the first deadline, merely set another and continue to work.

In 1954, Dr. Roger Bannister, the English physician, became the first man to break the four-minute barrier in running the mile. Within a short time, there were several runners who were consistently running the mile in less than four minutes, but Roger Bannister was the first.

By 1960, while the outdoor mile was consistently being run at times under four minutes, no one had yet beaten the four-minute barrier in an indoor mile. It was during this period that a young American runner, Jim Beatty, began to think about the indoor record.

By current standards, Jim really shouldn't have been a miler. He was too short, only five feet six inches tall.

That didn't keep Jim from being named the European miler of the year in 1960.

In September of 1961, Jim Beatty set a goal. He decided that he would become the first man to break the four-minute mile in an indoor race. Jim met with his coach, and together they planned a training program and set the time and place of victory. Beatty would break the record at the indoor games in Los Angeles on February 10, 1962.

The result is history. The time was 3 minutes 58.9 seconds. The achievement followed the classic plan: Beatty set a goal; figured out the time needed to accomplish it; decided what he had to sacrifice; developed a plan for success; and worked the plan.

Giving in Order to Get

Jim Beatty's story brings us to the fourth step in achieving financial freedom: determining what we are willing to sacrifice in order to attain our goal. How often we have heard the adage, "There's no such thing as a free lunch." It is important that you put on paper just what you are willing to give up to achieve your desire.

Quite often, one must sacrifice today the very thing he is striving to achieve tomorrow. It may be that you are seeking financial freedom in order to spend more time with your family, but find that for the short term, it is necessary to reduce available time in order to reach the goal. Evaluate your time, hobbies, pleasures and habits, and determine what you are willing to sacrifice. In order to obtain the time you need to give with your family while you attain financial independence, you may need to cut back on television, or golf, or the wasteful luxury of time spent inefficiently.

Plan Your Work; Work Your Plan

The next step is to develop a plan that will provide the wealth vehicle for achieving your goal. We will only mention the need to have such a plan, and to commit it to paper at this point. The remaining chapters of this book will deal with the selection of a wealth vehicle to achieve your financial goals.

Once the deadline has been set to reach your goal and the vehicle selected to carry you there, start immediately! There is no better time than now! Regardless of your age, you'll never be younger. Do not wait for a better time or better conditions. There is no better time than now!

See What Isn't There (Yet)!

While implementing the plan you have developed, allow your subconscious mind to work by consciously visualizing yourself as already in possession of the money desired. This is not to mean that you are to spend as though you had already acquired the desired funds, rather just picture yourself as though you already possessed them. Such visualization projects itself to your powerful subconscious mind, and to other people, creating the confidence and belief in yourself that you will attain your goal.

A friend of mine told of how he rose through the ranks of the U.S. Army from a raw recruit to a senior commissioned officer. My friend had enlisted in the Army to further his education and to see the world. After completing his basic training, the young solder was assigned to a military school where enlisted men, non-commissioned officers, and commissioned officers of all ranks attended the same classes.

It didn't take long for my friend to realize the difference of rank and what it meant. He determined that he would become a commissioned officer. As he walked to his classes each day, my friend pictured himself as an officer. In his mind, he rehearsed the actions he would take in given situations. He prided himself in wearing the proper uniform, even as a private, in accomplishing more than was required, and in obeying military courtesies.

The private studied the regulations to learn how to reach his goal. He then developed a plan of action and began immediately to implement it. My friend applied for Officers Candidate School, was accepted, graduated, and became a commissioned second lieutenant.

He later told me that it was not when they pinned on the bars of his rank that he became an officer. My friend had *BECOME* an officer while he was still wearing the uniform of a private, visualizing his goal on those walks to and from his lowly duty.

Visualizing oneself as in possession of the money or goal that is set does not mean we have already attained the desired goal. Here we practice the principle of delayed gratification. Even though we envision ourselves in possession of the desired goal, we wait until we have actually completed the work before satisfying our dsire.

Remember!

- Determine *WHY* you want freedom.
- Put your goals on paper!
- Assign dollar values or amounts needed to accomplish your goals.
- Decide when you want to reach your goal.
- Be willing to give up today what you want tomorrow.
- Develop a plan to achieve your goal.
- Follow your plan for success.
- Visualize yourself as already having achieved your goal.

Chapter Two

WHY DO IT BY YOURSELF?

There is a popular myth that the most successful people are those who achieve their goals without the help of others. The fact is that everyone needs some help to attain something truly worthwhile. The more aid a person receives, the greater the level of achievement that is possible and the quicker success is realized. This is particularly true of financial success.

John W. Galbreath, at the age of 85, is one of the most successful men in the world. His John W. Galbreath and Company has built office and housing complexes throughout the United States and Canada and in many other parts of the world. Mr. Galbreath owns the Pittsburgh Pirates baseball team. He relaxes at his 600-acre bluegrass horse farm, Darby Dan, located near Lexington, Kentucky, or at his 4,300 acre horse farm of the same name located near Columbus, Ohio.

Recently, Mr. Galbreath attended the dedication ceremony of an office complex in Lexington, Kentucky, which his company built and is part owner. Interviewed by a local newspaper concerning Mr.

Galbreath's philosophy of success, he said, "If you don't love people, you can have all the college degrees in the world, and you'll never be a success."

John Galbreath has found and used one of the most important keys to financial independence. Whether it be family, friends, employees or contracts, others can provide the positive reinforcement, money, skills and work that will make possible the financial independence that will allow you to achieve your goals.

Albert Einstein, after having formulated the theory of relativity, spent the rest of his life unsuccessfully trying to bring together two of the basic forces of nature: gravity, which holds the universe together; and electromagnetism, which controls such phenomena as fire, chemical reactions, and animal metabolism. Physicists have long postulated the existence of two other basic agencies working within the atom: the force binding the protons and neutrons, called the strong force; and the energy at work in decay and disintegration, the weak force.

The scientific postulation was that the weak force was composed of three particles known as $W+$, $W-$, and Z (degree symbol). The nature of these particles is such that, for two generations, they have defied all efforts to physically identify their existence. However, in early 1983, Italian scientist Carlo Rubbia, at the age of 48, appeared to have discovered the missing W particles.

Dr. Rubbia's genius lies not just in his scientific knowledge, but also with his ability to bring together a team of 134 European and American scientists, to guide their work, soothe their egos, and bring about the joint effort that achieved his dream. Of course, there have been mechanical advances since the time of Einstein, which aided Rubbia and his colleagues. Nonetheless, it was the Italian's capability as a leader which brought success.

You must learn to love what you are doing. The love of people and the love of work are the glue that holds success together.

A Wealth of Help in Your Family

When evaluating the participation of others in your path to financial freedom, the place to start is with your own family. Your family may be a help or a hindrance to your plans. The choice is yours.

K.K. Amini, chairman and majority stockholder of Sage Energy Company, is a man who has integrated his family into his successful pursuit of financial freedom. Thirty-eight years ago, Mr. Amini arrived in the United States from Iran, with $2,900 in his possession. Today, the Aminis are worth more than $120 million!

While many oilmen like to brag about the number of times they have gone under and had to start over, Amini has never come close to bankruptcy. Sage Energy has struck oil 164 times out of 164 tries over the past two years.

K.K. Amini encouraged his children to succeed at whatever they wanted to do, and to share his dream. Rex has acquired history, law and geology degrees; Susan, a Master's in anthropology; Ronald is a dancer with the Austin Ballet; and Michael is a pianist and Phi Beta Kappa graduate of Stanford. Not only have the children achieved their own goals, but each son participates in the management of the family company. "We all went off to school and didn't want to have anything to do with him for a while," Ron told Forbes Magazine, "but we all came back."

What are the keys to successfully integrating the family into the search for financial success? One is to share your dream with them. This is the most difficult step for most men and women. All of us want to be heroes in the eyes of our family. To share our goals seems to open us to the risk of becoming failures to those we care most about. What we don't realize is that it is those who are closest to us who are the most accurate judges of what we really are, and they love and respect us in spite of our shortcomings. It is the lack of a dream, or not sharing it, that is most likely to cause our dearest ones to lose respect.

Another key to family participation is to make specific plans for their inclusion in the work toward the goal of financial independence. How can you expect cooperative effort from someone who isn't included in the plan? Mr. Amini's sons returned to work for the family company because plans had been made for them to work in the corporation.

A third step in the inclusion of the family seems, at first, to be contradictory to the second. In order for a spouse, son or daughter to be effective in the family search for success, it is necessary that they receive encouragement to develop and realize their own dreams. How is this achieved? The answer is giving them time and freedom to choose. A person who does not feel successful in his own right is not likely to be effective in the cooperative role. If a family member doesn't feel that you are interested in his success, he is not going to be able to relate to yours. Thus, the planning for the inclusion of family members in the effort must contain sufficient flexibility to encourage achievement by the individual family member in areas of his or her own choosing.

Family participation in your goals is enhanced by seeking advice in the implementation and struction of the plan for achieving financial independence. This is especially difficult for men. The male is often taught that he should be all-knowing, all-powerful within his own family. It is important to realize that real strength lies in being open to advice. Obviously, not all advice should be accepted. The important thing is to create an atmosphere of honest cooperation, participation and membership in a joint effort.

If the output necessary for effective inclusion of the family appears great, so too are the rewards. There is no more efficient way of extending oneself than to have a family member as a representative—the more immediate, the better. This is practical, of course, only if the relative is committed to the same goals.

It is often difficult to recognize that those who are close to us may possess skills and abilities that exceed our own. This is particularly hard to see in our own children. Be aware of the special skills which your own family can bring.

Children must be trained; they must develop work habits. They must never be given monetary allowances. That's socialism. They must be taught to work for their own money, and therefore learn its value. Our children began to receive work responsiblities at six years of age. The child must be taught not to quit until the work is done.

Being relied on as a full-fledged contributor to the work helps the family member to develop a sense of self-worth and independence. Joan de Regt, senior consultant with an international market research company, is convinced that one of the major reasons children like to learn computer operations is that it gives them master of a skill which their parents do not have.

Rob Thompson, Jr., would have struck many parents as a problem. At 28 years of age, the ponytailed Rob was still working on his undergraduate degree in nuclear physics when he was informed that there would be no jobs in his field when he graduated.

While Rob was trying to decide what to do with the rest of his life, his parents interested him in helping them design a computer program for their insurance business. A brilliant computer systems designer, the young Thompson soon developed a program that was so effective the family decided to market the system to other agencies. Five years later, the Thompsons sold their joint enterprise, Redshaw, Inc., for $40 million.

As the family is made part of the undertaking and develops the feeling that this is a joint venture, they become better able to provide positive reinforcement. Being those we wish to please, the encouragement from them is more effective than from any other source.

One reward of including the family in the search for financial security is that they can provide a home atmosphere of rest and relaxation, a refuge from the toils and conflicts of the day. A place of escape is essential to the renewal of strength, so one can continue the effort to reach the goal.

How grand can be the family success? In 1763, two young men, each twenty years old, returned to Frankfurt in what is now Germany. One of the young men was a prince, William by name; the other an orphan who had been a bank apprentice and whose hobby was collecting rare coins. Not only was the young orphan poor, but he was a Jew and thus restricted in occupation. He was forced to live in the Jewish ghetto of Frankfurt and pay a "Jew's tax" each time he left the area.

Twenty years later, Prince William of Hesse-Cassels was one of the richest men in Europe, while the orphan had parlayed his knowledge of banking and his love of rare coins into a modest fortune. More importantly, the orphan had fathered five sons and developed a pattern for success that included them.

As the years passed, the fortunes of war reduced Prince William's wealth. He died in exile and today is but a footnote in history.

But the orphan adopted his surname from the red shield that hung above the door of his Frankfurt ghetto home and sent his five sons to the capitals of the world to expand the family business. To this day, the descendants of the orphan Mayer are among the world's most powerful bankers. Everyone knows the name— Rothschild.

Friends Can Help You Meet Your Goals

Al Horley and Johnny Johnson founded Vitalink Communications Corporation in 1980. The satellite earth station manufacturer had sales of $4 million in its second year of operation, with projected sales of $100 million in 1985. Johnson was a retired Air Force general and Horley worked in the federal bureaucracy. How could two men who'd spent most of their lives working for the government raise $26 million needed to start a new company? Simple. They shared their dream with friends. When the friends provided money and orders for equipment, it gave the two entrepreneurs borrowing power.

When reviewing what is needed for the successful implementation of your plans, friends should be among the first resources considered. There is often hesitation to approach those close to us with our dreams and goals. As with our family, we fear, "What if we should fail?" That is weak thinking. Who next to our family knows us better than friends? It is in spite of our weaknesses that they respect us.

Among the reasons friendships develop are: persons sharing the same goal; personalities or skills which complement each other; the existence of a mutual sense of trust. Aren't these the same qualities which would be of inestimable help in our work toward financial independence? Friends must not be overlooked in the striving toward our goal.

Seven years ago, Stephen Wozniak, now 32, dreamed about developing the equivalent of the Model-T Ford of computers. With some friends from a San Francisco Peninsula computer club and using existing technology, Wozniak scaled down computer size, making them inexpensive enough to be attractive to individuals as well as to companies.

At the same time, a twenty-year-old college dropout, Steven Jobs, returned to the area after wandering through India and experimenting with drugs and the free-life society. Jobs' and Wozniak's mutual interest in computers formed the basis of a friendship that resulted in the formation of a corporation, fulfilling Jobs' dream of selling the computers that Wozniak designed.

Last year, this company which resulted from the marriage of two friends' dreams had sales of $583 million and a stock market value of $1.7 billion. It is known as Apple Computer, Inc.

Employees Who Care

There is another group of people who may play a significant role in your plans for financial success—employees. While it's easy to fall into the "I'm paying, so they better do as I say," attitude, that is definitely not the way to gain effective support.

In 1982, two similar businesses ended under very different circumstances. While Wicke's Home Improvement Centers filed bankruptcy, Payless Cashways, Inc., earned approximately $20 million. Analysts attribute Payless' success to the fact that their store managers are paid bonuses of 3% of the store's pre-tax profits, plus up to 25% more if net margin goals are met. This is in addition to better-than-average base salaries.

The United States trucking industry is undergoing a period of intense competition caused by the deregulation of the industry. Profits are down for many over-the-road carriers and several are expected to file for bankruptcy. One exception is Overnite Transportation Company, the eighth largest in the country. It is posting operating profits greater than ever.

Credit for this unusual performance is given to the company's founder and chief executive, J. Harwood Cochrane. Overnite's non-union operation boasts payroll costs that are the lowest in the industry. Cochrane does things like structuring runs so drivers can have maximum time to be home with their families at night. He believes that if an employer is genuine and sincere, maintaining an open door policy, employees will work "like it's a big family, and not a big company." Employees are most likely to be effective in helping you fulfill your goals when they share your dream, and can expect to share in the rewards of success.

Who You Know Can Be Helpful

Contacts differ from friends and acquaintances in that the relations between contacts is based on the real or anticipated ability of the parties to help each other achieve separate goals. Such a relationship may develop into friendship, and, given time, are likely to do so, but the initial impetus is one of mutual benefit.

Maurice Tempelsman, owner of Leon Tempelsman & Son, is one of the leading diamond traders in the world. Much of his success is due to his uncanny ability to develop and maintain contacts, both to his advantage and that of his associates.

Tempelsman was born in Belgium where his father, Leon, was a flour mill owner and trader of commodities. The family immigrated to New York as the Second World War began. Since Leon Tempelsman had left behind most of his wealth, he began work as a diamond broker.

The younger Tempelsman wanted to enter politics or teaching, but eventually studied business and entered the family company. Apparently Leon had prepared a place for Maurice, and it paid off.

First, Maurice coupled the family fortunes to international politics. In 1950, at the age of 21, he persuaded the U.S. government to buy industrial diamonds for its reserve of strategic materials, using European currencies produced by Marshall Plan purchases. He then convinced European companies to sort the stones as a means of creating jobs. Tempelsman became the broker, buying diamonds from African producers and supplying them for processing to the European sorters.

This operation formed the basis for Tempelsman's move into barter exchanges that provided savings to the government and profits for him. He traded raw materials from African countries for surplus agricultural products from the United States' government.

As these deals were being conducted in the early 1950's, Tempelsman saw that the colonial era in Africa was coming to an end. To him, change was not a threat, but an opportunity. The 27-year-old diamond dealer hired Adlai Stevenson as his attorney, taking the former governor with him as he began touring the emerging African nations. Mr. Stevenson was immensely popular in Africa at that time and provided an entree that could not be duplicated.

With the contacts developed in this maneuver, he proceeded to build, carefully following the rules for relationships that guided his conduct. Andrew Young, former ambassador to the United Nations, is reported to have described Maurice Tempelsman as honest, candid, and non-threatening. No matter how common corruption and payoffs may be in a country, Tempelsman insists he never indulges in those practices to develop his important contacts.

The successful diamond dealer has continued to follow the rules which have made him not only a business associate to the leaders of Africa, but also a trusted confidante and counselor, even in countries with frequent changes in government. Tempelsman even followed his father's example and induced his son, Leon, to join him as manager of their retail operation in the United States.

Watch Yourself!

What is it that keeps us from effectively integrating others into our search for financial freedom? Two stand out as most common: the desire to control others, and jealousy. In order to successfully work with others, we must understand that the greatest control comes from one who feels no need to control. *THE GREATEST CONTROL COMES FROM ONE WHO FEELS NO NEED TO CONTROL!* If you are committed to accomplishing a task, regardless of what others may do, others are free to join you in the enterprise.

Jealousy is one of the most self-destructive forces known to man. No one is successful until he learns that another's accomplishments do not diminish his own. Only as others achieve their goals are they free to be effective participants in your endeavors.

The intelligent integration of family, friends, employees and contacts into the undertaking of achieving financial security is one of the most important keys to achieving that goal.

Remember!

- Others can be helpful in reaching your goals.
- Let your family help you achieve success.
- Don't sell short your family members' abilities.
- Include friends in your plans.
- Make employees part of the team.
- Look for acquaintances who can help you achieve your goals.
- Don't let jealousy or a desire to control others drive away those who would help you.

Chapter Three

YOU ALREADY HAVE MORE THAN YOU THINK

You know where you want to go. You've translated the goal into a dollar figure. You've set the deadline for arrival. Now, it's time to select the vehicle for accomplishing your goal.

Some people say any old jalopy will get you where you want to go. That may be ture. But, remember, your time of arrival depends on the efficiency of the vehicle. Though you may begin toward your goal in a Model T Ford, you'll be passed up by someone speeding along in a supersonic jet. So is your financial vehicle as important.

To select your vehicle, begin by taking an inventory of resources available to you. Money is the first item on the inventory. How much money do you personally have to devote toward your desire, and how much can you readily identify as being available to you through other sources. Remember! Lack of money should never be a reason for abandoning a plan!

It is important to have a realistic estimate of how much money you have available to develop your plan. That amount will have an impact on which vehicle you select or the amount of time you must plan for to reach your goal.

How Are You Fixed for Cash?

There are two basic measures of money we may use to determine your ability to pursue plans for financial security—net worth and cash flow. Net worth is determined by subtracting liabilities (what one owes) from assets (anything owned which has value for exchange). Cash flow is that amount of money that may be expected to be received on a regular basis, such as salary, rental income, interest.

To establish net worth, one must begin by listing assets. What are assets? Webster defines assets as "anything owned that has exchange value." The place to start is by listing money: savings and checking accounts, dollars in money funds. Then, list non-money current assets, those items of value for which there is a ready market, such as stocks, bonds and U.S. Savings Bonds. Gold coins, silver and gold certificates would also qualify as current assets.

After completing your list of current assets, begin a list of other assets such as real estate, loans to others, art objects or family heirlooms, jewelry, personal property, automobiles and the cash value of insurance policies. Personal property can be estimated at 25 to 30 percent of the value of your home, exclusive of art, jewelry, and unusual items such as a personal computer, large-screen television, or an expensive stereo.

Family heirlooms and art objects are often held with no idea as to their true value. It might be worthwhile to have these items appraised, both for a more accurate net worth statement and for purposes of insurance.

For several years, Bob refused to give his wife the money to have the old cabinet she had purchased at a garage sale refinished. He was convinced it was a piece of junk. With Bob away on a two-week business trip, Margaret sent the piece to a refinisher, who correctly identified it as a valuable antique. The $15,000 that Bob and Margaret realized from the sale of the cabinet provided the funds that allowed Bob to leave the agency where he worked and start his own real estate firm.

To complete the process of establishing net worth, it is necessary to determine liabilities, those obligations one is legally bound to fulfill. There are occasions where you may feel a moral obligation to repay a real or imagined debt, but these should not be included in determining net worth.

Current liabilities are normally considered to be any debt that is due within one year. Items to be included are credit card balances, short term loans, installment purchases, and the like. Mortgages, educational loans, and other obligations with payback periods in excess of a year are considered long-term liabilities.

After your liabilities have been listed, they are subtracted from the assets, and the result is your net worth. Net worth becomes a measure of capability to take on additional debt, in that it indicates the existence of possessions which could offset that debt, if necessary. It should be noted that net worth does not indicate the availability of cash. Current assets, less current liabilities, is a better indicator of available money.

There are two ways to increase net worth—to increase assets or decrease liabilities. In most cases, the maximum financial benefit will be obtained by decreasing the liabilities.

There are times when the liabilities may exceed the assets, resulting in a negative net worth. Many of us find this to be the case as we begin our plans to attain financial independence. This does not mean that we are in a position that makes us unable to borrow money. It is then that cash flow, that second measure of money available, comes into play. Net worth does not necessarily give an indication of cash available. It does give an indication of assets available to offset the liabilities of a loan.

The Ins and Outs of Cash

In the short term, cash flow is much more important to an evaluation of financial ability. The time you may spend in efforts to secure financial freedom which does not produce immediate cash (most such time spent in those initial months, or even years, does not) is governed by the availability of cash to meet your living expenses.

Salaries, dividends, interest payments and rents received are examples of cash inflow. Living expenses, rent, mortgage payments, bills, and loan payments are examples of cash outflow. If, in a given time period, there is more coming in than is going out, there is positive cash flow. Conversely, if more is going out than is coming in, there is negative cash flow. No matter what your net worth may be, negative cash flow is trouble.

Planning your personal cash flow needs is especially important to the successful implementation of your plan. Not having what you feel you need financially is a grinding worry and its psychological impact will transmit itself to others.

Morgan dealt with this problem by keeping his needs to a minimum. When he graduated from college, the young man decided he would become successful by brokering real estate investments. In order to do this, Morgan approached one of the most successful real estate investors in the country and agreed to work at whatever job he was assigned if the investor would teach him how to put together real estate syndicates.

For the next five years, Morgan found himself working in various cities across the country as an attendant in parking lots owned by his mentor. His income was so small that a hamburger was a special treat. He couldn't afford to get married. But he did learn the real estate business. In the four years following his tutelage, Morgan was able to put together real estate syndicates which made him a millionaire by the time he was in his early thirties.

A very simple procedure will help you analyze your status concerning cash flow. Draw twelve columns the length of a piece of paper. At the head of each column, put the month of the year, beginning with the current month, at the left hand column.

Draw a line across the middle of the page and, for each month, enter expected income above the line and expected output below it. When you total these figures, you'll have a good indication of months in which you may have more income than payments, and months when you may need to save for obligations that exceed income.

An evaluation of your cash flow may cause you to see that you may do whatever you please with your time. On the other hand, you may discover that you need to find time in your plan for financial freedom that will not interfere with the time you currently need for producing an income.

Skills are Worth Money!

C.B. Vaughan knew a lot about skiing. In 1963, he set a world downhill speed record, traveling at 106 miles per hour. During the next five years, Vaughan thought about ways to turn his skills at skiing into a business of his own.

Vaughan finally decided to go into the business of designing and making ski clothing. The young entrepreneur had never studied design or clothing manufacturing, so he read a book on making patterns. Soon, he bought a pair of ski pants, took them apart to see how they were made, and made his first pair of insulated ski pants. They were awful! It took him ten tries to come up with a wearable pair of pants, but today, clothing from Vaughan's CB Sports, Inc., is the most sought-after ski wear in the world.

Ted Carter was 37 years old and the owner of a successful investment firm when he suddenly realized how bored he was with his work and the people who went with it. Ted loved to entertain interesting people at his New York lake country home, so he sold his business and turned his home into a retreat for high-paying guests.

Vanessa Evans reached her mid-thirties, bored with her job as a paralegal. She had been promised more responsibilities, but more young, fresh-from-law-school attorneys were added to the staff. Finally realizing that her job was a dead end, she began taking stock of what she wanted to do with the rest of her life.

Somehow, she knew that becoming an attorney with the prospects of handling divorce suits and debating property line disputes was not for her. Vanessa was told by a job counselor that she was "getting to the age where she would be hard to place" and that she had just about reached her potential income level in the job where she was. The counselor urged Vanessa, at age 33, to be happy and stay put.

Angrily, Vanessa left the office, refusing to be limited by the tunnel vision of a job counselor. So what did she want to do with the rest of her life? She had many capabilities, but Vanessa couldn't decide what she did well enough to make a career of it. Finally calming down, the determined woman decided to start from square one. What had been her best subject in school? The answer was English. She began evaluating the career choices. Teaching held no appeal, nor did advertising. It came down to two choices: Vanessa could either read other peoples' work, or write her own. When she made the conscious commitment that she should be a participant in life, rather than an observer, Vanessa went back to night school and polished her writing skills. Before long, she was happily earning her living as an author.

The stories of Carter, Evans, and Vaughan illustrate the second item on our inventory: skills that we possess or can acquire. If you are unsure of your own hidden talents, now is the time to take stock. On another sheet of paper, note your hobbies and skills, beginning with things you do best. You'll be amazed at all the different things you already know how to do. The list should give you guidelines for pinpointing your own custom-made vehicle for success.

Remember!

• To inventory your money, measure net worth and cash flow.

• You can increase funds available by increasing income or reducing outflow.

• Look for hidden value in things you own.

• Special skills can help you toward your goals.

• Lack of money should never be a reason for abandoning a plan.

Chapter Four

IDEAS: YOUR MOST VALUABLE ASSET

Ideas are the seeds which germinate in action, sprouting verdantly into our fondest dreams. Without an idea, there can be no action, no working toward goals. Therefore, we must pay close attention to any ideas which might develop into that vehicle for financial independence.

You may have noticed by this time that the sequence for your inventory is not set in concrete. An idea for a new business may come to you before you know how much money you have available. In fact, a good idea will attract money that you may not have listed as a possible source. Your thoughts on the solution to a problem may generate the desire to develop a new skill. Don't worry whether the chicken comes first, or the egg. Just be certain that your inventory considers all of the items covered.

Idea sources that can trigger the means for success are limitless. We will review three broad categories to help in analyzing your idea resources:

- Those ideas that are generated by problems.
- Possibilities for doing what someone else has

done, but doing it in such a way as to fill a niche they have missed.

• Implementing the idea of another who may not have the resources or desire to fulfill it.

Negatives are always balanced by positives, in life as well as in nature. Napoleon Hill stated, "Every adversity, every failure and every heartache carries with it the seed of an equivalent or greater benefit." Learning to use difficulties as the source for positive input is the key to success.

A Black Man's Problem

Some problems are inherited. John Johnson was born a black man in 1919 when being black was really a problem. He attended high school during the Depression. The Depression was a problem. He lived with his widowed mother in the Chicago slums and they were poor. That was a problem, too.

Today, John Johnson is one of the richest and most powerful black businessmen in America, with a net worth estimated at $100 million. That is *NOT* a problem. How did he do it? John Johnson allowed the negatives of his situation to generate positive ideas.

Because he was black, one of the few professional opportunities open to him was with a black-owned insurance company. After working successfully with the company for six years, Johnson talked the owners into allowing him to utilize their 20,000-name mailing list, borrowed $500 from his mother, and mailed out offers for discount subscriptions to his first, and as yet unpublished, magazine, "Negro Digest." The idea for the magazine was generated by Johnson's awareness of his "problem" of being black.

There were 3,000 returns to the mailing, each with $2 enclosed, providing the funds for printing the magazine. In order to get a news distributor to take the magazine, he got his friends to ask for "Negro Digest" at newstands and then bought the magazines back from them, convincing the dealers that there was a demand for the publication. The re-purchased copies were then re-sold. This operation was repeated in New York, Detroit and Philadelphia. Within one year, Johnson was selling 50,000 copies a month.

In 1945, three years after starting "Negro Digest", the more popular "Ebony" was launched, followed by "Jet". Today, an estimated half of the adult black population is reached by Johnson's publications. It is virtually impossible to sell to the black consumer market without him.

After successfully expanding into broadcasting with radio stations in Chicago and Louisville, Johnson again ran into one of those "problems" he finds so rewarding. For 25 years, "Ebony" has sponsored the world's largest touring fashion show, Fashion Fair. Johnson was having trouble finding cosmetics in shades dark enough for some of his models. After unsuccessfully approaching both Estee' Lauder and Revlon to produce black cosmetics (each now does), Johnson decided to produce his own. Today, Johnson's Fashion Fair cosmetics are sold by over 1,500 department stores in the United States, Canada, Africa, Great Britain and the West Indies, with sales of over $30 million last year, producing more than $12 million in revenues. John Johnson now believes that the idea generated by the cosmetic "problem" may turn into his greatest success yet. Don't try telling John Johnson about the problem of being born black.

Just the Boss's Kid

For Bill Witter, as for many others, the key to success was in recognizing that he had a problem, which opened the way for the idea leading to fulfilling achievement. Few would have recognized that working in the firm founded by his father was even a problem. The common response by outsiders was, "He's got it made." However, working in a family firm usually causes problems both for the individual and for the company. The second or third-generation family member suffers from a nagging guilt, "Did I get that promotion just because of who I am?" The firm suffers because of the insecurity of such managers.

Dr. Srully Blotnick noticed in his twenty-year study of some 2,000 individuals, most of whom were businessmen, that "the companies run by executives who inherited their position were characterized by the highest level of destructive competition among its top management." Note that this refers to inherited situation, not where the family builds the firm together.

One of two sons of company founder Dean Witter, the younger Bill worked his way from registered representative to head of institutional sales, learning the brokerage business as he progressed. At the age of 36, he decided that, for him, success would not be spending the next 20 years waiting to take over the firm which bore his father's name.

Noting that many of his friends were working for themselves, Bill Witter founded his own brokerage firm, specializing in servicing institutional clients with information on small business. He later merged this operation with another company and, today, heads his own organization, William D. Witter, Inc., managing the investment of $375 million for pension funds and other institutional investors. Rather than becoming an insecure manager following a set line of progression in the family firm, Bill Witter has aggressively pursued and achieved success on his own.

Who Would Buy a Railroad?

Sometimes a whole industry seems to be one gigantic problem. After all, who would want to own a railroad? Murray Slazberg, that's who. Since he talked his father into buying him his first bankrupt railroad, convincing him that, if necessary, they could sell the scrap iron to cover the investment, Murray Slazberg has been making money from railroads. He was able to run that first purchase for over 20 years—in the black. Since then, he has repeated that performance several times, becoming a millionaire in the process.

Money from Mistakes

The apparel industry is beset by problems—changing styles, overproduction of items that don't sell as well as expected, labor problems, delays. It takes 18 months from designer to display racks in retail stores. What seemed a sure winner at time of order may, 18 months later, turn out to be a real dog. What to do with the mistake? Call Sy Syms. Mr. Syms' stores produced an after-tax profit of $10 million on sales of $115 million last year. He buys the manufacturers' mistakes in name brand merchandise, keeps his overhead low, pays cash, and makes money from others' problems.

Too Tough for a Woman?

At the age of 40 plus, with no business education, she was on her own with a child to support. While many would be overcome by the problems, Mary Kay Ash saw only opportunity. In just 19 years, her Mary Kay Cosmetics grew to over $235 million in sales in 1981, increasing four times in the last three years. It was her own delicate skin care problems which gave her the idea for one of the most successful new companies in recent years.

A-Sailin' We Will Go

The OPEC-inspired fuel cost increases put many businesses in a bind. The trucking industry was particularly hard hit. But the problem of increased transportation costs gave a 36-year-old college administrator an idea. Greg Brazier began building a sailboat in his back yard. Not your ordinary sailboat, but a 70-foot steel cargo ship with two 65-foot masts, seven sails and a 20-ton load capacity.

Greg's ship makes a daily round trip voyage from Long Island to Connecticut, covering the 16 miles in two hours, compared to a three-hour, 120-mile each-way trip for trucks driving to the same destination. Using wind to power his carrier, Brazier's costs are about 50% of those of the truckers. A small diesel engine takes over when there is no wind, but, so far, he is using only about 15 gallons a week at a cost of less than $25.00.

A Grandmother's Dream

Pansy Ellen Essman had a problem. The 42-year-old grandmother found it nearly impossible to hold onto her squirmy granddaughter, Letha, while giving her a bath. The situation continued to plague Mrs. Essman until one night, she dreamed that she was holding her granddaughter in a sponge pillow. The dream was so vivid that Mrs. Essman got up to make note of it.

(Please note that good ideas are lost because people fail to take note of them while they are fresh in the mind. Always keep paper and pencil available, even by your bedside. The subconscious brings forth some of our most productive ideas during sleep. If the thought is strong enough to awaken you, it is important enough to write down.)

For the next 13 years, Essman worked to eliminate

one obstacle after another. Money was in short supply so she continued working as a parts inspector at an electronics firm, producing the infant "Bath Aid" evenings and weekends. To keep overhead down, she moved the operation into a chicken coop on her mother's farm.

It didn't happen overnight, but, by 1975, at the age of 55, Pansy Ellen Essman was able to leave her $3.50 an hour job with the electronics firm and begin nationwide distribution of her invention. When larger companies began to produce a similar product, Essman brought in a marketing expert as president and made him a partner. He expanded the product line and improved distribution so that today the Pansy Ellen brand name is found on a full line of nursery products, and Essman Company has sales of over $5 million a year with a 15% profit margin.

Makes a Sick Company Well

Roy McKnight's idea for success was to take over the company that had caused his problem in the first place. In 1976, McKnight was the 55-year-old president of a manufacturer's representative firm whose pension fund had a large investment in drug manufacturer, Mylan Laboratories. Informed of the impending bankruptcy of Myland, McKnight decided to attempt a salvage of the pension plan's investment.

What McKnight discovered at Mylan was a nightmare. Inventories were overvalued by $2 million, more than $400,000 in withholding and social security taxes were past due; almost $2 million was six months past due to creditors; and 320 production workers were on strike—and there wasn't even a union. If those problems weren't enough to discourage him, McKnight had no experience in the field of generic drugs.

For each difficulty, Roy McKnight saw a possibility. With his experience as a manufacturer's representative for several different products, he soon developed a sound knowledge of the generic drug business. For finance and development, he brought in experienced managers who had faith that the situation could be turned around. To alleviate the immediate financial situation, McKnight talked the board members and company officers into personally guaranteeing a loan and increasing their investment for a total of more than $1 million. The workers' grievances were settled and the force went back to work.

It took only six months for the once sick company to change from red ink to black. Today, five years later, sales are approaching $50 million and the future looks brighter than ever for Myland Laboratories, all because Roy McKnight had a problem with one of his pension fund investments—and decided to do something about it.

Value in Loss?

For a bankrupt company, a long-term lease on property no longer used is definitely a liability, right? Not according to Michael Swerdlow, a bright New Yorker, who, with his percing gaze, long graying hair, and gaunt face set off with a Van Dyke beard, looks more like a modern-day Merlin than a real estate entrepreneur.

The typical reaction of a bankrupt retailer has traditionally been to renege on his leases, leaving himself liable to claims from the landlord. After all, to them the lease is just another bill with no positive value.

Swerdlow looked at the problem differently. Leases negotiated at old rates considerably below current market rate, he felt, should be worth the capitalized difference to the new tenant. As an example, if the old rate was $5 per square foot and the current market value is $30 per square foot, then the difference should be of value to a new tenant.

Of course, there were problems with the idea. Most leases contain standard clauses that provide for the landlord's cancelling the lease if the client goes bankrupt. What to do when the law is against you? Swerdlow went to court and changed the law. The courts agreed that the landlord should not profit from the tragedy of the tenant.

Michael Swerdlow's idea has been worth hundreds of millions of dollars to companies undergoing bankruptcy, and, in the process, has made him a millionaire several times over. He has salvaged cash from old leases for Food Fair, J.W. Mays, Korvette, and from Wicke's, the largest retailer ever to file a Chapter 11 bankruptcy. He is now looking for ways to apply his idea to the leased planes of Braniff and other financially-troubled airlines.

Helping the Helpless

There is no problem of our age that has taken a more devastating toll on the individual, the family, and society than drug abuse, and no single drug is more widely abused than alcohol. One out of every ten Americans in the work force, about 14 million, have a serious drinking problem. In spite of the need, an estimated less than 15% of those who could use assistance are being helped.

Many in the medical profession were troubled by the lack of attention given by the profession itself. The prevailing attitude seemed to be that no one was an alcoholic unless he drank more than his doctor. The "Catch 22" is that physicians have the highest rate of alcoholism of any profession.

In 1972, Lee Karns was faced with another problem. He was the owner of two failing hospitals plagued by that industry's problem of under-utilized beds. Karns, a former health care consultant, conceived the idea of treating two problems at once. He would provide treatment for alcoholics in his hospitals, utilizing the excess bed capacity. Because the treatment was provided in a hospital, insurance coverage was extended to many who were being encouraged by their employers to seek help, with the company picking up the tab.

Today, Karn's Comprehensive Care operates in 100 hospitals across the country with 53 additional units waiting to be opened. Revenues for fiscal year 1982 were over $73 million, with profits close to $8 million. Karn's ownership percentage has made him a millionaire—all because of an idea born of problems.

Find an Empty Spot

Another source for "success ideas" is what I call "identifying niches"—that is, not the invention of a product or thinking up a new service, but rather providing a service to a segment of the market not currently served, or making a product in a different size than is presently available. In some cases, the filled niche may be a coupling device that brings together two existing products. The most important thing to remember when you are looking for *YOUR* niche is: Find a need, and fill it!

You Want to Buy a What?

For anyone familiar with the automobile industry, now would certainly not seem to be an auspicious time to purchase an automobile manufacturing plant. Don't tell Steven Blake that. At a time when financially-troubled Chrysler required government aid to survive and DeLorean's dream of a moderately-priced super sports car went up in smoke despite heavy financial backing, Blake just laid down $5 million to buy the United States' smallest automaker, Avanti Motor Corporation.

When the Studebaker Corporation was forced to close its South Bend Automotive Division in 1964, the Avanti was saved from extinction by two local auto dealers. The two believed that there would continue to be a market for the futuristically-designed sports sedan, which, in spite of its being assembled by hand, carries a moderate price tag of $25,000 to $30,000. It was a good move. Sales have increased each year, with a healthy 15% increase in 1982 to its current production of about 200 cars per year. At a time when the major auto manufacturers are having a hard time moving their inventory, Blake is in the enviable position of having an order backlog of about 25% of his annual production. The secret of Avanti's success? Finding the right niche.

It's Impossible

Everyone knows it's impossible to make any money in the steel industry in the United States today. For one thing, labor costs are double those in Japan and ten times the wages paid to South Korean workers. However, in spite of paying blue collar salaries that average more than those paid to U.S. workers in large steel companies, tiny Nucor Corporation of Charlotte, North Carolina, earned over $13 million on sales of $379 million in the first nine months of 1982. By melting scrap steel in small, technologically up-to-date facilities known as "mini mills," Nucor is able to produce specialized steel products in quantities too small to be efficient in the larger production facilities of traditional U.S. mills.

Kenneth Iverson, president of Nucor, attributes the company's success to the utilization of modern equipment and techniques, and the incentive system that forms the basis for wages. Some workers receive bonuses that are greater than 200% of their base salaries. The system results in an average Nucor worker producing over 800 tons per year, compared with an average of only 350 tons per year for workers in the larger steel companies.

Even IBM Can't Do It All

It was in 1974 when Richard Greene identified the niche that was to lead to his success. Greene was an account executive with IBM, servicing one of the computer giant's largest customers. While reviewing the customer's computer operations on a routine service call, Greene noticed a non-descript box sitting right in the middle of the computer room.

Labeling on the box, he knew, indicated a non-standard product normally manufactured in numbers of one or two. Investigating back at IBM, Greene discovered that the box was a computer/peripheral switch and that IBM had installed over 6,000 of the so-called one-of-a-kind items. It was then Greene saw his niche.

The computer/peripheral switch is a vital piece of equipment that allows users of large computer systems, such as those in airlines, the defense establishment, insurance companies, etc., to rapidly move memory and terminal capability from one main frame to another. The net effect is to keep everything on line all the time. Because of its importance, customers are willing to pay a premium for a reliable computer/peripheral switch, thus making the item less subject to the constant downward pressures on the prices of computer equipment.

Greene was anxious to start his own company, but knew that he did not have the engineering background necessary to raise enough capital to go into competition against giant IBM.

Selecting his next best option, Greene joined a small electronics manufacturing company and, utilizing their engineering expertise and capital, developed a computer/peripheral switch that was faster and had a greater capacity than IBM's. In a short time, Greene was heading a new division overseeing production and sales of the new switch. Within three years, he saw sales of the company double.

In spite of his success, Greene still longed for a company of his own. In 1977, just as his new division was beginning to peak, he took a second mortgage on his home and began a computer consulting business under the name, Data Switch. While advising data processing managers how to make their systems more efficient, Greene continued to preach his gospel that the switch was inevitably one of the customer's weak spots because IBM wanted it to be. An efficient computer/peripheral switching system, he maintained, allowed the data processing manager to use his company's assets with maximum efficiency, thus reducing the need for newer equipment with greater capabilities.

By 1981, Greene's abilities as a consultant had become sufficiently established that he was able to raise $1 million from five private investors to develop a dual computer/peripheral switch that was superior to anything currently available. Since then, Greene's Data Switch Corporation has grown to approximately $16 million in sales for 1982, with earnings projected at around $2 million. The net result is that Greene's 40% ownership has made him a millionaire.

Who Says It's a Language Problem?

To the stranger idly reviewing television selections in a U.S. city with a large, Spanish-speaking population, tuning in Rene Anselmo's channel might provoke a mild case of culture shock. To begin with, the screen may be filled with giant letters, "SIN." No, he hasn't stumbled across a blue movie—just the network symbol of the National Spanish Television Network, originally founded under the name, Spanish Information Network.

It was in 1960 that Anselmo, recognizing the need for Spanish language programming, attempted to sell programs produced for the Spanish-speaking population to the major networks. In those days, it was a hard sell situation. The only times the stations or networks seemed to have available for this specialized programming were on weekends or late night.

Recognizing that the viewing habits of his Spanish-speaking audience were basically in the same time frame as those who spoke English, Anselmo began his network with the purchase of one television station in San Antonio, Texas. Today, his network has more affiliates than NBC, with five owned and operated stations, plus 33 UHF stations and 168 part-time Spanish stations. Additional revenues are generated by a Spanish language cable pay TV channel which is carried by 150 cable systems. Revenues in 1982 were about $80 million with net income estimated at $4 million.

The future looks bright for Anselmo's niche in the television broadcasting industry. The Spanish-speaking population in the United States is estimated to be increasing at a rate that is seven times faster than the population at large. To serve its growing constituency, SIN utilizes a satellite capability that allows it to pick up direct transmissions from abroad, including such events as world cup soccer, and to transmit its signal with maximum economy.

Medical School Profits

For years, the medical community has been accused of limiting the number of doctors by controlling admissions to medical schools. Both the American Medical Association and the Association of American Medical Colleges are represented on the committee that accredits medical colleges. The two have often been accused of taking a position that limits the number of colleges able to train physicians, in order to control competition in the field. Although such charges have never been substantiated, there is no doubt that the demand for a medical education far exceeds the supply available in the United States.

After the son of a friend was denied admission to medical school despite his excellent academic record, Bob Ross, a wealthy New Yorker, decided that there was a market for a good medical education, taught in English and geared for entry into practice in the United States. Ross decided to set up his own "free enterprise" medical school.

Ross University began classes on the Caribbean island of Dominica in 1979. Today, hundreds of its alumni are in residency training in U.S. hospitals. Ross contends that, prior to the establishment of his facility, U.S. citizens who had been unable to enter a U.S. medical school had to go to Mexico, Italy, or Spain to obtain a medical education. His facility, he says is staffed with English-speaking teachers, most of whom are American and know the U.S. medical system.

When Ross University graduates enter the United States to practice, they are treated as any other foreign-trained physician, required to pass a special federal examination and meet state licensing standards. Meeting these requirements allows them to practice in most states.

Look for the unfilled needs in existing industries. Check for the different size package that may be needed, the special switch, the low volume item that doesn't have sufficient demand to attract the major manufacturers. Look for a niche to generate the idea that will carry you to success.

The Computer Chip Farmer

J.R. Simplot appears an unlikely candidate for a computer manufacturer. What would an Idaho high school dropout who built his fortune on the profits of a pig farming operation know about random access memories and 64K chips? For those who are familiar with the Idaho entrepreneur's career, however, it comes as no surprise that Simplot put together a team of rich farmers and businessmen to finance Micron Technology's move into the highly-competitive field of computer chip manufacturing. Simplot was never one to hesitate to use others' ideas, so when he heard of the Parkinson twins' idea, who, along with their friend, designer Douglas Pittman, believed they could develop a more efficient 64K computer chip, he put together the financing.

The obstacles to the development of this chip by the small company seemed insurmountable. The Japanese had taken the lead in the development of these chips with the help of a $400 million research and development effort, funded jointly by major corporations and the Japanese government. Major governments, universities, and the most innovative high technology computer companies in the world had spent some $5 billion over the past few years trying to develop the chip that tiny Micron had in mind.

Within a year, Micron had developed a chip that, in the words of one industry expert, is the "best combination of size and capacity" on the market.

At the first of this year, Micron Chairman Ward Parkinson and his twin brother, Micron President Joseph Parkinson, were able to present a new breakthrough: The reduction of the bare chip to about half the size of the best-selling Japanese and American-made chips with the same capacity. The smaller chip size means lower manufacturing costs, thus reducing prices to consumers.

The chip's layout design is the work of Douglas Pittman, a 32-year-old college dropout who is termed by those exposed to him as a genius in the layout of computer chips. Major savings were realized by bypassing expensive tests which had been considered essential in the development of chips. In addition, Pittman designed his product with sufficient tolerances to allow its use in the manufacturing of a personal computer. While the market for 64K RAMs (Random Access Memory) is only 30% of the total production, it is the fastest-growing segment of the industry.

J.R. Simplot recognized that *IT DOESN'T HAVE TO BE YOUR OWN IDEA THAT PROVIDES A VEHICLE FOR SUCCESS!*

It was the founder of TV Guide magazine who provided the original idea for a popular magazine based on one facet of the electronics industry. Today, that idea has sparked dozens of entrepreneurs, publishing magazines on or about personal computers. The latest tally indictes that there are at least a half dozen of these publications devoted solely to the IBM personal computer.

Rags to Riches

The idea of selling used clothing is probably as old as mankind itself, but that has not stopped a resurgence of the sale of used clothing everywhere, from fashionable Christie's Auction House in Manhattan to Bogie's in New York's East Village, where unwashed clothing is piled in a 10-foot high pyramid on the floor.

While the Salvation Army and Goodwill Industries have long sold used clothing as a means of helping the poor, Harvey Schefren, a New York accountant, used the idea to build a multi-million dollar fortune.

In 1962, Schefrem founded Noamex, Inc., with the purpose of supplying poorer countries of the world with the cheapest clothing available. For less than $100 per ton, Schefren shipped used clothing around the world from his gigantic New York City warehouse. Items that even the poorest of Americans were unwilling to wear found a ready market in many of the poorer nations of the world.

In the late 1960's, Schefren, along with his younger brother Gary, decided to expand their distribution system. They selected some of the more usable items and marketed them as pre-washed jeans, shirts, and jackets to outlets located near universities, to be sold to college students who thought dressing "poor" was in vogue.

In 1980, the Schefrens realized that the "vintage" clothing market was expanding. A review of their inventory convinced them that as much as 20% of their products could qualify for resale in the United States. The Schefrens founded Antique Boutique which, with 11,000 square feet, is the largest used clothing store in the world. Old Hawaiian shirts from the '50's, used wool sweaters, and retired overcoats are snapped up by the 7,500 people who visit the establishment each week. Last year, the less-than-poor shoppers at Antique Boutique spent over $3 million. When those sales are added to the $8 million a year revenues of Noamex Inc. in its overseas venture, it is obvious that the Schefren brothers are not doing badly on someone else's idea.

Remember. The source of an idea is immaterial. Whether it comes from a problem you encounter, a friend or acquaintance, or is generated by an unfulfilled need, the important thing is to identify the idea that will lead you to the vehicle of success.

Don't Re-Invent the Wheel!

All of the above success stories are about people who have found a need to be filled, and have filled it. It's important to remember that they didn't necessarily go out and find something new.

Popularized by business legend and lore, most people feel their road to success lies in finding that something new. The truth is that those marvelous stories are rare, and most success comes from staying with things that have proven themselves. For success, find something that's already working and jump on it, rather than always trying to re-invent the wheel!

Remember!

- Ideas are your greatest resource.
- Look for opportunity in problems.
- Find a niche that needs filling.
- Don't be afraid to use another's idea.
- Always write down your ideas.
- Make special note of ideas that come while relaxing or dreaming. Keep a pad by your bedside to note such thoughts.

- For every negative, there is an equal or greater positive.
- Look for something that's already working and jump on it!

Chapter Five

THINKING STRAIGHT!

Attitude! It can shoot you straight to the stars—or dump you into the depths of despair. Nothing we've talked about, not even the importance of a great idea, is as important as your personal attitude. For, even with the best idea, if you think negatively about it or about yourself, you are doomed to failure.

You Can if You Think You Can

Leo Rautins is a strapping 6'8" giant who speaks with a gentleness that belies his size. His friendliness and easy-going manner made the young man a popular figure on the University of Syracuse campus. Observers credit Rautins for the national ranking and successful seasons of the Syracuse basketball team on which he played. Rautins' aggressive defense and uncanny accuracy have made him a sure-fire selection in the first round of the pro-basketball draft. Not an unusual story, except for the fact that Leo Rautins is one of the few Canadians to play big time college basketball in the United States.

It wasn't an easy road for Leo from the streets of

Toronto to a starting role at the University of Syracuse. Although he grew up with a love for basketball, it appeared his chances were ended when doctors discovered that Leo, at the age of 11, had developed a spinal disease that had deteriorated his spine and was causing his left leg to atrophy.

"No more basketball," the doctors told the youngster, but Leo believed he could play. And play he did. Soon the young Canadian was being talked about throughout the country as he dominated high school basketball games. At the age of 16, Leo was selected for the Canadian national team.

Canadian newspapers wrote articles about the young superstar, always qualifying their praise with the note that there was no real Canadian opposition to prove his skills. "He'll never make it in big time U.S. college basketball," they said. "There's no Canadian role model for him to follow."

But U.S. college coaches *DID* come to see Leo Rautins play. He *DID* receive offers to play with major U.S. universities. Leo Rautins *DID* play in the big leagues of United States college basketball and became a dominant force. When questioned about the reasons for his success, Rautins smiled and responded, "I knew I could do it."

Leo Rautins had developed the single most important attitude in achieving success. He learned to believe in himself. Success has come to many people, with many different problems. There have been successful young people, and successful old people. The blind have overcome their lack of sight, cripples their lack of mobility. Many have risen from poverty to positions of responsibility and power. Others have overcome the temptations of great wealth and a life of ease, selecting instead the life of service to their fellow man. *BUT NO*

*PERSON HAS ACHIEVED ANYTHING WOR-
THWHILE FOR HIMSELF OR FOR OTHERS
WITHOUT DEVELOPING A SINCERE BELIEF IN
HIS ABILITY TO ACHIEVE THE TASK BEFORE
HIM.*

The story of Leo Rautins should not be unusual, but unfortunately, it is. In many ways, our society has a tendency to reward mediocrity. In our desire to provide education for all, we sometimes discourage the bright student. Phrases like, "Don't make Johnny look dumb," or "You don't want to be a know-it-all," are too often repeated to a bright youngster who is just following his natural inquisitiveness.

Those who have achieved wealth or power are often portrayed in the press as having reached their goals by cruelly exploiting those less fortunate. Business leaders are portrayed as amoral. Politicians are regarded as rogues. Public figures who express patriotism are ridiculed as sad relics of the past. It sometimes appears that there is a national media obsession with destroying heroes.

The net result of this atmosphere is that most of us live with doubts about our own ability to accomplish our goals and even the desirability of reaching for our dreams. We allow the negative forces about us to instill the seeds of self-doubt, and end up with a "settle for" attitude, isolating ourselves from the world, trying not to make waves.

Fortunately, we can change this situation. You can develop a strong belief in yourself. You can take on that task with the assurance that you can accomplish it. You can realistically assess your own abilities and inspire others to help you in the achievement of your goals.

Believe in Yourself

Carl Hathaway discovered the benefits of believing in himself and, today, Carl Hathaway is a happy man. Oh, yes, gone are his days of lunches in an oak-paneled executive dining room with crystal and china. Gone are the morning trips on the New Haven Railroad as one of the business "elite" making the daily trek from the posh Connecticut suburbs to a mid-town Manhattan skyrise. Today, Hathaway rides his bicycle to his small office overlooking Connecticut's Five Mile River. Lunch, more often than not, will be a cold sandwich eaten on a paper plate. But Carl Hathaway is a happy man.

Just over two years ago, Hathaway had to contemplate the embarrassment of having been "kicked upstairs," at New York's mammoth Morgan Guaranty Bank. In the early hours of the morning, Hathaway looked out the window of his new 45th floor office, viewing the lights of New York and contemplating his future. He was approaching 50 years old. Obviously his peers no longer trusted his investment decision expertise. He had been removed from the day-to-day operation of the trust department which he had headed since he was 35 years old. He knew he could "retire in place" and enjoy the perks of a high-level executive position with one of the nation's major financial institutions. But, as the early morning sun rose over the East River, Carl Hathaway made a decision. He decided to believe in himself.

Today, Hathaway isn't the only one who is happy with that decision. GTE Corporation, Rockwell International, Champion International, IBM, and Alcoa have all invested more than $25 million with Hathaway and, during 1982, saw those pension fund investments increase by over 30%. Today, Hathaway moves confidently about his office making investment decisions on everything from Mexican food to medicine packaging. By believing in himself, Carl Hathaway found success.

On Becoming Positive

But you may say, "I don't believe in myself. How do I find belief in my own abilities?" There are two keys for creating an atmosphere that allows you to believe in yourself: Surround yourself with positive input; and remove yourself from negative thoughts.

You've taken one step in providing positive input to create a good self image—you are reading this book. Literature which provides a positive, uplifting message is one of the most important sources of teaching and learning to believe in yourself. Set aside a time each day to read the writings of men like Norman Vincent Peale, Robert Schuller, and Napoleon Hill. Teach yourself to relate to the positive stories which can be found in the business news. Also, I find it personally helpful to listen to positive thinking tapes when I'm involved in a task that does not involve my complete attention.

Associating with positive people creates an atmosphere that allows success. Seek out people who are achievers. Make it a point to be around them. Listen to their advice. Watch them as they relate to other individuals and learn from such encounters.

Creating an atmosphere that will lead to a climate of success calls not only for the conscious decision to introduce positive inputs, but also requires the purposeful removal of negativity. I am associated with some highly successful people who refuse to read a daily newspaper because of the pervasive negative message they find there. Many of my successful friends consciously avoid television newscasts because the concentration of demoralizing features is detrimental to their success. Both of these positions are extremes that you may or may not find necessary to adopt, however they do point out the importance of being selective in what you concentrate on. Negative input will have its impact on your thinking and it will make it difficult for you to believe that you can accomplish anything worthwhile.

It's important for you to develop an awareness of attitudes in those people with whom you are in constant contact. A person who is constantly critical, continually complaining, one who is always pointing out others' faults will leave a negative impact on you. Stay away from such people. Don't allow someone else who has made a decision to not succeed to steal your dreams.

The Ostrich Syndrome

Thinking positively about your activities and abilities does not mean ignoring reality. A healthy positive mental attitude is always based on a realistic assessment of the facts. A healthy self-confidence faces the situation as it is and changes the negative. It does not ignore challenges, pretending that they will go away. It does not stick its head in the sand. Circumstances do not become what we want them to be only by saying that it is so, but as the result of positive affirmation *AND* work!

Dream but Don't Cheat

During the 1970's, Med General, Inc., was one of the fastest-growing medical electronics firms in the country. Today it no longer exists. In May of 1979, when corporate stockholders and officers met for the annual meeting, the future looked bright. The brilliant doctor-inventor, Robert Ersek, who was majority owner and founder of the company, praised the abilities of the company's manager, Jerald H. Maxwell, and proclaimed him as the man responsible for Med General's amazing growth. Maxwell's report presented 1978 sales as showing a 70% increase over the previous years, with earnings up 50%. The next year, he promised, would bring even more dramatic results. The stockholders showed their approval with several interruptions of applause.

Only four short months later, Maxwell could be found sitting in his office, a beaten man, his company and his world collapsing around him. When the final audits were completed, the emerging picture was not that of a thriving medical electronics firm, but that of a company who had shipped items not ordered, run up sales to companies who had not paid, failed to allow for bad debts, and generally operated in a manner where the figures reflected dreams rather than facts. In fact, Med General's outstanding sales figures were often pure fabrication.

Those closest to the situation placed the blame on Maxwell's refusal to accept facts, deciding instead to create figures that reflected his goals, rather than to change the problems that were impeding the desired results.

A realistic self-confidence will allow you to deal with the facts. It will help you to find means to overcome obstacles, ways to solve problems, and methods to remove impediments to your success.

The Family that "Yea's" Together, Stays Together

I'm a strong believer that, in the nuclear family, a man should be the head of the house, giving the unit leadership and direction. The woman is his co-partner, equal but serving a different role as manager of the household assets and supporter of the combined effort to achieve success. You may disagree with me. That is certainly your right. But I would be remiss if I did not inform you that my experience has indicated that when husband and wife have settled in these roles in a harmonious cooperation, their chances for success appear to be many times greater than when such conditions do not exist. Whether the reasons for male leadership are caused by social pressures or exist in natural law is really not important. The fact is that most men feel guilty if they are not exerting leadership and most women resent a lack of leadership being exhibited by their partner. The existence of either guilt or resentment in the family will erode the self-confidence that is essential to the achievement of success.

The Importance of Co-Workers

Why is the attitude of co-workers so important to our success? Every time I think of this question, I am reminded of a Chevrolet dealer in Rome, New York, who enticed me into his office. There had been an ad in the newspaper: Car salesman wanted. I saw a chance to change my career and improve my life. Selling automobiles would have been a step up from my job at Sears, where I had been doing the best job I knew how. However, I was continually looking for a chance to improve my situation. But, the Chevrolet dealer turned me down flat. "You stutter," he said. "You can't sell cars."

He was right. I couldn't sell cars—for him.

Obviously I had some abilities. I was to go on to earn millions of dollars in my early working years—money made by selling ideas and things. When my Rolls

Royce collection was recently displayed on network television, I wondered if the old Chevrolet dealer was watching.

A few weeks later at the Ed Maxwell Ford dealership, I met Stan Joslyn. He said, "Why don't you come on over and sell cars for me?"

I dutifully repeated what the other car dealer had told me. "I can't sell cars," I replied. "I stutter."

"How do you know you can't sell cars?"

"I just applied for a job at the Chevy garage. They told me I couldn't sell cars."

"Young fella," he said, "you're the young guy up at the Sears store who sold every one of my salesmen a lawnmower, aren't you? I've been in business many years, and I know that you're a salesman."

Stan Joslyn, the Rome, New York, Ford dealer was right. I did well selling automobiles over the next few years. However, there is no doubt in my mind that I would have failed had I been associated with people who were convinced I could not do it.

Competing with Yourself

For achievement, it is necessary to have an atmosphere which allows single-minded concentration. A work place filled with disharmony, dissatisfaction, or destructive competitiveness makes it impossible to concentrate on the job at hand.

"But," you may say, "aren't all successful people competitive?"

Yes, successful people are competitive, but they are not competitive with others. If you are to achieve your highest goals, your accomplishment must not be measured against what others may do, but against what you know yourself capable of doing. Competition thus is striving to effectively utilize your own capabilities to their maximum. Working in an atmosphere where others seek to rise to the top by ridiculing the accomplishments or abilities of their co-workers makes it impossible to concentrate on the tasks to be done. If you recognize yourself clawing and biting your way to the top, you need to change. Immediately! Start "giving to the world the best you have," knowing that "the best will come back to you."

The Customer Is King

Another key to accomplishing what we want is to develop a proper attitude toward our customers.

"I don't have any customers," you say.

Every product or service has an end user. For a while, assembly line workers in U.S. auto plants seemed to forget those customers they never saw. Before long, the effect of their neglect was noticed in the showrooms of car dealers across the country. No amount of smiling by the car salesman was able to offset the sloppy workmanship in the automobile. The old adage, "Never buy a car that was made on Monday or Friday," ceased to be a joke. The situation is changing, but not without the loss of thousands of jobs.

While we're talking about customers, it's important to remember that since they are the end consumers of whatever products we may offer, we must be certain that any products we choose to sell must be:
1. Good merchandise.
2. Priced right.
3. Needed by the customer.

When we keep those three criteria in mind, we're well on our way to success in the merchandising field.

A Smile Can Work Wonders

I haven't always had a chauffeur. Some time ago while traveling, I stopped at a truck stop late at night. I'd been working late, but was determined to return home because of appointments there the next morning.

I wandered into the restaurant to get a cup of coffee, hoping it would help me stay awake for the remainder of the trip. The cafe was filled. Every table was occupied and the counter had no empty seats. As I approached the counter, there appeared to be no waitresses anywhere. Suddenly, from behind the counter directly in front of me, up popped a waitress, both hands filled with dishes. Her face was almost touching mine. We stood there startled for a moment, then she grinned and said, "Hi. What'll ya have?"

"I'd like a cup of black coffee, to go, When you get time."

"It won't take a minute," she grinned, and scurried off to deliver the dishes to a nearby table.

It was apparent that she was the only one waiting on a restaurant full of about fifty people. I knew it would be a while before I was served. I was wrong. In just a few moments, she was back with my coffee.

"Here you are," she smiled. "Just pay the cash register," and off she went to take care of another customer.

As I stood at the counter to pay for my coffee, I noted with wonder at how one friendly waitress was serving all those people and creating such an atmosphere of relaxation despite the arduous task before her. As I drove through the night, I noticed with amazement that the attitude of that smiling waitress seemed to drive the tiredness from my bones. She certainly made it a more pleasant trip home.

Special Delivery

Houston-based Sysco Corporation is just one of about 2,000 firms in the business of wholesaling food to institutions and restaurants, but there is a difference. Sysco is considered the most profitable in the industry, Why?

A favorite story to explain the phenomena is told by Sysco chairman, John Baugh. The chef of a posh Houston restaurant believed that he had everything under control for a special lobster dinner one Saturday evening. Suddenly, ten unexpected guests arrived. Where could one find lobsters at 5 p.m. on Saturday afternoon? The chef called his Sysco representative at home. As the story is told, the salesman arrived within the hour with the extra lobsters he had purchased at a local gourmet shop. According to the legend, the salesman even placed the lobsters on the grill.

It is this attention to customers' needs that allows Sysco to charge a premium for its service to 90,000 nationwide customers. "We don't just sell food," says Chairman Baugh, "we sell peace of mind."

Even as I'm writing this book, I'm thinking about you. Am I saying the things that will help you in your search for success? Am I presenting my thoughts so that they are understandable? Will you find this product useful to your needs, and be able to recommend it to others?

Each task should be approached with the end user in mind.

Control Your Circumstances

Not only are our attitudes concerning people important, but also our bearing toward the circumstances in which we find ourselves. Do we approach each day with the knowledge that for every problem there's a counterbalancing opportunity?

In a major business news magazine, the editors recently reported, "The appetite for bad economic news seems voracious. Most people seem determined to ignore the favorable signs." Do circumstances determine your outlook on life, or do you, by a disciplined, positive approach, turn your surroundings into opportunity?

Recession? Don't Participate

For most cash intensive companies, 1980 and 1981 was a period of slow business and lower return on equity. Not so for Miami's Ryder System which lease and rent trucks. This company, the largest of its kind, boasted record returns on record sales, and a return on equity of nearly 20%.

The 1974 recession had pushed the company to the brink of financial collapse, causing a major change in management. This time, Ryder was prepared. When the depressed economy caused a slump in truck leasing, Ryder cut its rate by 50%. The rate reduction caused an increase in equipment utilization that more than offset the loss in higher fees.

When Ryder's auto transportation subsidiary began to falter due to reduced auto shipments, Ryder expanded by purchasing other car transport companies. The resulting increase in contracts allowed trucks, which had previously been delivering cars one-way and returning empty, to pick up additional deliveries in the drop area, returning home with a product for a dealer nearby. Ryder was challenged by its circumstances, and found a way to meet and benefit by the challenge.

Just Been Fired? Good!

James Kennedy was 34 years old, married, and the father of five children. He had advanced rapidly in his profession, becoming managing editor at the magazine where he started as a reporter, then moving to the top of his department in the consulting firm with whom he was associated.

On Friday before the upcoming Memorial Day weekend, Kennedy was advised that his services would no longer be required. For the first time in his life, Kennedy had been fired.

He went home to discuss the situation with his wife. By pinching pennies, they decided they could manage without work for six months before having to call for help from relatives.

Kennedy had long dreamed about starting his own business as a public relations consultant, but he frankly admitted he was too scared to take the step. After the firing, of course, circumstances (which only appeared to be negative) made his dream closer than ever. Things fell into place so well that in the first month of operation, Kennedy earned only $50 less than he had made the previous month working for someone else.

Kennedy's consulting company led to a newsletter. The newsletter has resulted in speaking engagements, and, while Kennedy declines to discuss his income, his office is a new two-story affair, complete with solar heating and a kitchen. James Kennedy has the look of a contented man as he talks of his seven children, six of whom live within a few miles of his New Hampshire home, and his grandchildren, three of whom attend a day-care center run by his wife, Sheila—all because of his attitude about being fired.

Will the circumstances of life control you? Or will you find, in those same circumstances, opportunities for achievement? It's up to you.

The Ultimate Attitude

There is one other area of attitude that I have found personally important in achieving success. That attitude is one of belief in the Benevolent Supreme Being who is the dominant influence in the world. Unless you have faith in God, it is difficult to imagine that you could find any reason to seek success in the first place.

Whatever your faith, make sure that your conduct is governed by the principles of your religion. Find time to meditate and renew your spirit.

Remember!

- You can if you think you can.
- Create a positive atmosphere around yourself by reading positive books and listening to positive tapes.
- Seek out and spend time with positive thinkers.
- Avoid negative people.
- Believe in yourself even when others don't.
- Assess your strengths and weaknesses realistically.
- Develop a program to overcome your weaknesses.
- Surround yourself with co-workers who have a positive attitude.
- Compete with your own goals—not with others'.
- Make your customer king.
- Smile, smile, smile.
- Control your circumstances, rather than letting the circumstances control you.

Chapter Six

SQUEEZE, SQUEEZE, SQUEEZE!

Squeeze the buck! Some of you reading this are going to say, "He sounds like a miser!" That's not the kind of squeeze I have in mind. Think about it for a minute. When you want to make orange juice, you squeeze the orange. You don't throw the orange against the wall and hope you might catch some juice.

Sounds ridiculous, doesn't it? And yet, that's just the way some people manage their money. At the time Free-spending Freddie picks up his paycheck, he has no idea which of the bills he is going to pay that day. There is a stop at the grocery store for the week's groceries, without a grocery list, of course. Maybe it'd be fun to throw in a steak to surprise the wife. After all, she deserves it, he rationalizes. A stop at the filling station for the weekly fill-up. An attendant points out one of the tires is bald. Can't drive on bad tires. There goes another $50.00.

Freddie arrives home, hands what's left of the paycheck to his wife, and is absolutely amazed when she asks him how she is to pay the bills with this little money. After all, he didn't waste anything. The purchases were all necessities. Or were they? The food was necessary, but which food? The gasoline was necessary, but how much? And to go where? The tire was obviously needed, but when should the purchase have been made?

Learning to successfully manage the money we have is essential to financial independence. In the parable of the talents, Jesus Christ pointed out that the person who learns to manage what he has will be given more, while the person who cannot manage what he has entrusted to him will find that even that is foolishly frittered away.

An imaginative person can double the power of their income. I learned how to do this as a young man. It was the first year in my own business. I was often on the road; expenses were high. Then I struck on a formula that would double my mileage and double the value of my dollars—simply stay in a motel only every other night.

Having driven all night, I would arrive in town, check into a motel early in the morning and sleep in. In the afternoon and evenings, I would keep appointments and hold meetings, getting to bed as soon as possible that night, and sleeping in until noon the next day. I squeezed two nights sleep out of the motel.

The next afternoon, I kept all my appointments and had another night full of meetings. But this time, I hopped into the car instead of the motel. A long night of driving was ahead of me. I didn't mind. There would be a motel bed early the next morning. Besides, I was really going someplace. The sacrifice didn't hurt. It was even fun. A little extra inconvenience had doubled the purchasing power of my money.

Dexter & Birdie with Art Linkletter.

William Shattner of "Star Trek" fame and Bob Hope congratulate Dexter & Birdie Yager.

Cheryl Prewitt-Salem with Dexter & Birdie.

To Dexter Yager
a great leader & Inspiration
to all who know you.
Warm personal regards,
Pat Robertson

Pat Robertson with Dexter & Birdie.

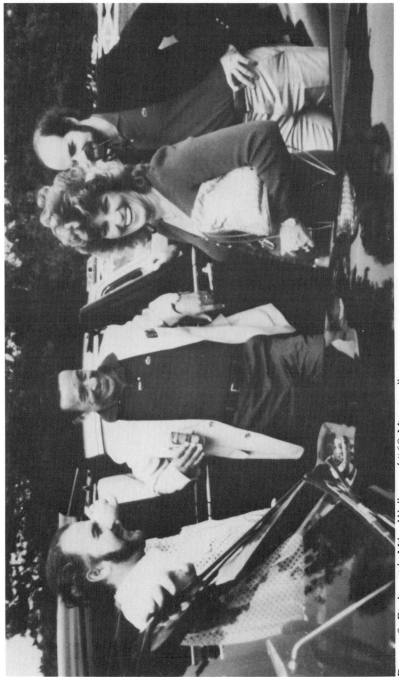

Dexter & Birdie with Mike Wallace of "60 Minutes."

*ex,
irdie —
I think we're all
lookin' better all
the time — I know
you are!
I love ya —
Pat —*

Pat Boone with Dexter & Birdie.

Dexter and Birdie with Gerald Ford.

Mrs. Jimmy Carter with Dexter & Birdie.

Dexter & Ronald Reagan.

Dexter & Birdie with Alan Thicke.

Brenda Lee with Dexter & Birdie.

Tom Smothers with Dexter & Birdie.

There are two basic reasons for learning to manage the money we have. The first is good stewardship, the principle behind the parable of the talents. If you don't learn to manage what you have, even if you make a lot of money, you'll never be financially secure. Financial independence is the combination of income to meet our wants as well as our needs, and the ability to manage that income.

The second reason that it's important to live within our means is that it relieves us of the worry of financial pressures. The person who must continually worry about how he's going to pay his bills is unable to concentrate on the tasks that will allow him to achieve success. Not only do such pressures lay waste to the process of creative living, but there is nothing more destructive to a person's self-image than the knowledge that he is not financially providing for his family.

Things don't have to be that way. You *CAN* learn to manage your money.

The purpose of this chapter is to help you develop money management with well-planned goals as a step on your road to financial independence.

Budgeting Your Money

"Oh, I know how to budget. I just figure up all my bills. Pay them. And live on what's left over." Sound familiar?

What is a budget, really? A budget is a statement of *PLANNED* income and expenditures, to help us achieve a financial goal. And, actually, a budget doesn't start with bills, but with essential expenditures.

Take a piece of paper and, at the top, write, "Monthly Budget." On the first line of the left-hand side write, "Family Income," then list the income that the family expects to earn over the next month from all sources. Total it, and put the total figure in the right-hand column, toward the right-hand side of the paper. Draw a short line and then, on the right-hand side of the paper, write "Essentials." Under that first list, enter, "Food." Over to the right, put the minimum amount you feel is necessary for food for one month. Next, list shelter. Under "Shelter," list your utilities expenditures and the rent or mortgage payments.

The next item under "Essentials," should be clothing. No matter what his occupation, a man should have one good-quality suit of a cut that will not go out of style, medium lapels, dark in color. The budget should also provide for the woman to purchase each year at least one good quality dress.

One of the comments I often hear is, "My teenagers are growing so fast, I just can't keep them in clothes." I'm a firm believer that teenagers should earn money to purchase their own clothes. No matter how much money the family has available, the parents are responsible for teaching children the value of the dollar, as well as a sense of responsibility. You would be amazed at the amount of money that a teenager with only parttime jobs can earn at baby-sitting, yard work, and other miscellaneous jobs.

Requiring the young man or woman to be responsible for at least a part of their clothing needs is certainly not cruel. To the contrary, it can help them develop a sense of self-worth.

Absolutely every teenager should pay for his own fun!

The next item under "Essentials" is transportation. This is where you list car payments, a monthly allocation for insurance, gasoline allowance, and a maintenance allowance. If your car is paid off, don't automatically go shopping for a new one. It's my belief that, unless you use your car daily in your business which requires you to drive long distances, you should purchase a car with the intention of driving it until it stops. If you anticipate needing a new car, set aside an allowance to save for it so that you can pay cash. We'll talk about car purchases a little later.

I also list my church contributions under "Essentials." You may do as you choose, but I have found that regular tithing is an essential expenditure for me. It reminds me that I place God first in all areas of my life, including finances, which, for many of us, is the most difficult area to release to Him.

The next step is to total the "Essential" expenditures, subtract them from the "Income" and make a subtotal of the amount remaining. Hopefully, there will be some left. If the "Essential" expenditures exceed the income for the month, obviously either the expenditures will have to be reduced or the income increased.

It may be necessary to consider taking a second job. Another alternative is moving to a smaller home, or one with lower utility costs.

After considering essential expenditures, list individually all of the bills you must pay. Be sure to note beside each bill the number of months that you must continue to pay it before it will be retired. When the monthly bill payments are totaled and subtracted from the income, any remaining amounts will be considered for investment. We'll talk about investments in the next chapter.

"I don't have enough money left to pay all of the bills," you may say. "Should I consolidate my bills with a new loan?"

No! Another loan is not the answer to your situation. I do not mean to imply that you should not pay your bills. Just debts are a moral as well as financial obligation. Here's my advice for handling the situation:

1. Review your expenditures on Essentials and make certain that you are budgeting the absolute minimum for each item. If you can meet your bills by eating beans and rice for a couple of months, or delaying some clothing purchase, or putting off a planned trip, do that.

2. If your bills are such that short-term reductions in "essentials" will not allow you to make all of your payments, list all of the bills. Note the total amount due and the amount of the monthly payment for each; then allocate the money you have available so that you can make a payment on each bill every month.

3. Send a letter to each creditor, explain that you have overextended yourself, and that your finances are such that you can make payments in the amount you have allocated until the bill is completely paid off. There are some creditors who may react with a letter stating they will sue if you don't pay immediately. A short note telling that creditor that, unless he accepts the repayment plan, you will be forced to file a bankruptcy is usually sufficient. Most creditors realize that they are unlikely to receive payment in full if bankruptcy becomes necessary.

4. Be sure that you follow the agreed-on repayment schedule. Your creditors are making an allowance for you. It is imperative that you follow your original agreement with them.

Some of you will say, "Well, if I do that I won't be able to get any additional credit." You don't *NEED* any additional credit. The "charge it" mentality has sidetracked more people from their road to success than any other single item. Period. Get in the habit of paying cash. Recognize that if you can't pay cash you probably can't afford the item anyway.

Don't get discouraged if you find in the first few months you don't follow your budget exactly. Learning to follow a budget is an acquired habit. Keep trying. You can learn to follow your financial plan.

Budgeting Your Time

"Time is money!" How often have you heard that said? Time is not money, but it is the essential ingredient needed to make money.

What do I mean by budgeting time? The nature of time makes its planned allocation even more important than the budgeting of money. Money lost can be found; time lost is gone forever. Money saved can be banked; time saved must be immediately allocated or it is lost. The thoughts, ideas, and emotions felt in a given moment can be recalled, but the moment itself, once it has passed, is gone forever. How strange it is that many people who are religious in the budgeting of their money have never realized the importance of the proper planned use of their most precious commodity, time.

The value of planning one's time was impressed upon me many years ago when I was working as a salesman in upstate New York. My job required me to call on an average of 30 to 40 customers every day. Most of my clients' places of business were located on busy thoroughfares. I found that by backing my car into a parking space I could save between 30 to 45 seconds in getting back on the road after completing my call.

Thirty seconds doesn't seem like much. When multiplied by the number of calls I made each day, it totaled nearly an hour. Those 30 seconds added an additional half day's work each week, and, through the course of the year, improved my productivity by 25 days!

Andrew Carnegie's Key to Efficiency

Many years ago, according to legend, a young Charles Schwab approached the great industrialist Andrew Carnegie with the claim that he had a secret method for improving Mr. Carnegie's personal productivity ten times over. Andrew Carnegie listened and was so impressed that the young Schwab became the financier's most trusted adviser. He was later entrusted with the operation of the U.S. Steel Corporation, at the time the largest business in the world.

What was it that the young Schwab imparted to Andrew Carnegie?

Simply this: At the beginning of each day, list the ten most important tasks to be performed during that day. Rank them in order of their importance, with the most important task at the top of the list. Concentrate on each job until it is completed, then cross it off the list and move on to the next item.

Whether the legend is true or not, I do not know. I do know this: the plan works.

In using this simple plan to improve my efficient use of time, I have discovered a couple of principles that have made this system more useful. The first is that if any item on the list becomes distracting to me when I am working on something I thought was more important, I will move the distracting job to the top of the list and get it out of the way so that I can concentrate on what else needs to be done.

In addition, I have found that it is most effective to start each new day with a new list. I will review the list from the previous day, selecting those items that still need to be accomplished, adding new tasks, and ranking them according to urgency. Interestingly enough, some items that seemed very important when first considered never get to a place on the list where they are accomplished, and in time become so minor that they are dropped from my list.

Doing Two Things at Once

The effective use of time demands single-minded concentration on the task at hand—IN MOST CASES. Yes, there are exceptions. The most obvious exception is utilizing travel time that might otherwise be lost to accomplish a compatible task.

The proper use of travel time was impressed upon me when I was employed in the sales job I have referred to before. One of my responsibilities was to review billboard advertisements that the company had placed, making certain the signs were in good repair and were displayed at the place and during the time for which we had contracted. By scheduling my sales calls in such a way that I drove by the location of our billboard advertisements, I was able to accomplish that particular task without the expenditure of any additional time.

Plan effective use of travel time. If you are driving, use a tape player to listen to some training or motivational material. If you are riding on public transportation, make certain to provide yourself with useful reading material.

Listen to Me!

At this point, let me add that there is one area where it is extremely important that you concentrate on one task and one task alone. *WHEN INVOLVED IN A CONVERSATION AND THE OTHER PERSON IS SPEAKING, CONCENTRATE ON LISTENING AND ON NOTHING ELSE!*

For most of us, this is a difficult task. Instead of listening, the average person finds himself thinking of what he has said or what he is going to say or how what he is saying is affecting the other person's conversation.

There is probably no greater single cause of wasted time than the failure to listen. In my experience, developing effective listening habits will improve your productivity every bit as much as utilizing Mr. Schwab's idea of listing daily tasks.

How does one develop good listening habits? I have found the most effective way is to listen not only with ears but with pencil and paper. Remember those days in school when listening seemed to be so very important? Accurate retention of facts was increased merely by taking notes.

It seems strange that a person who has spent 12 to 16 years of his life developing good listening habits in school would find it so hard to apply the same principles in becoming a success in life. Make it a point to listen!

Ring, Ring, Ring!

In Japan, the telephone is called a "ding/wa," a word which actually sounds like the rude, intrusive, electronic interruption it is. And, rather than answering the telephone with a soft, "Hello," the Japanese answer with the words, "Mushi Mushi," which, to the foreign ear, comes across as the good idea of "Hurry up; let's get this over with."

While I'm not suggesting that it's necessary to be rude in telephone conversations, it is necessary for you to control the telephone, rather than letting it control you.

"But," you may ask, "what can I do about all those calls I receive?"

Set aside a specific period of time each day to return calls and to make necessary calls. Don't allow phone interruptions at other times, unless you have made a specific schedule to receive one. Of course, there are emergencies for which you would wish to be interrupted, but these are usually few. If you work where you have no secretary or receptionist to intercept the calls, set aside certain periods of the day during which you disconnect the phone. People who really need to get in touch with you will call back.

The telephone can be a very useful and efficient business tool. It can also destroy efficient use of time. Control the telephone. Don't let it control you. You are not a slave.

Remember!

• Time is the most valuable commodity you have; treat it with respect.

• Plan your expenditures of time and money so that they help you reach the goals you have set.

• Start immediately by implimenting your budget of time and money.

• There are two ways to increase the money available to you:

1. Increase your income.
2. Decrease your outflow.

• If your current bills and living expenses exceed your income after cutting living expenses as much as you can, pay each creditor a set amount each month until you retire that debt.

• Use Andrew Carnegie's Key to Efficiency.

• Don't be a slave to the telephone.

• Budgeting is an acquired habit. Don't be discouraged if you try to budget your time or money once or twice and fail. Keep trying.

Chapter Seven

A-SHOPPING
WE WILL GO!

Many people approach shopping with about as much concern as they would approach a nursery rhyme. A hunting we will go, a hunting we will go, hi-ho the dairy-o, a hunting we will go!

One can never attain financial independence without developing shopping discipline.

A friend of mine recently told me of his experience as a young sailor stationed in the Far East. The prices for cameras, stereos, tape recorders, and other electronic paraphernalia were so attractive in the military exchange system that he went deeply in debt purchasing them. "I almost went bankrupt saving money," he said.

That turned out to be a useful lesson for the young sailor. Unfortunately, many of us find ourselves in similar positions and never seem to learn.

In today's world, a whole science has been developed to entice you to buy. Every time you walk into a store, the deck is stacked against the possibility of your leaving that store without purchasing something that you don't need or did not intend to buy. Loss leaders, (items actually sold below the cost the retailer paid for them) are used to entice you into the store. High profit items are strategically placed to maximize the chances of their catching your attention and your subsequent purchase. A whole industry has grown up by finding clever ways to advertise products so you'll buy them.

All of the resources of mass media advertising and Madison Avenue psychology are geared toward making you an impulse purchaser. Unless you learn to discipline your buying habits, you will find yourself continually broke no matter how much money you make.

Plan Your Shopping

Mary Ann is a 35-year-old divorcee living in Cincinnati, Ohio. With two small children, the $25,000 annual income she earns as a buyer for a local department store is her sole source of income. On the other hand, Larry is a 40-year-old medical equipment salesman living in Denver, Colorado. Last year, Larry earned over $50,000. His wife, June is a school teacher and added $25,000 last year to the family income. Larry and June have no children.

Listening to Mary Ann and Larry discuss money matters, you might first believe that both were experiencing the same difficulties in finances. Mary Ann complains about there never being enough money. Larry describes himself as being part of the affluent poor.

Yet, as you examine their financial situation, you find a distinct difference. Mary Ann has a savings account, her "rainy day fund," as she calls it. In that account, she keeps the equivalent of three months' salary in case anything should happen to her. In addition, she has a private retirement program and a regular stock investment program. Mary Ann regularly puts money aside to help with her children's education.

Larry, however, is always complaining, "I just can't save a dime."

It's ture. In spite of Larry's and June's better-than-average salaries, there is nothing left by the time all the bills have been paid. The reason for this difference became apparent in conversations with the two families. Larry was proud of the amount of money that he made. His spending philosophy was summed up in his own words, "If I like it, I buy it."

Conversely, Mary Ann was careful with her shopping habits. "I never go shopping without a shopping list," she said. "And I never buy anything that's not on my list. I've found that I can have anything I want if I plan for it."

In spite of her limited income, it's very likely that Mary Ann will be able to retire comfortably some day. When the time comes for Larry to retire, he'll probably still be complaining about never having enough money to do as he wishes.

How does one develop the planned shopping habit?

1. Plan what you buy.

Mary Ann had developed what is perhaps the most important habit in developing shopping discipline. She always made a list before going shopping. Your shopping list should include two columns: first, the item you are going to purchase, and, secondly, how much money you can afford to spend for that item

2. Determine why you are making the purchase.

Jeff is a 35-year-old stockbroker in Dallas, Texas. "Every year I buy one custom-made suit, for which I pay between $500 and $700. I know that I could pur-

101

chase a good-quality suit off the rack for less than half that money, but just the knowledge that I am wearing the best gives me confidence when dealing with my clients."

Bud is a 55-year-old plumbing contractor in Memphis, Tennessee. "I spend top dollar to get the best quality tools for my business. I pay a premium for that little extra quality, but I figure the cost in time for me or one of my employees every time a tool breaks makes the extra money I invest well worth it."

Jeff purchases his suits to fulfill a psychological need that he feels makes him more productive in his profession as a stockbroker. Bud purchases his tools to fill a functional need which maximizes his effectiveness as a plumbing contractor.

This leads us to two basic reasons for purchasing: to fulfill a function use or to fulfill a psychological need. Both reasons for purchasing are valid.

It's interesting to note that both Jeff and Bud purchase quality items to fulfill their needs. Jeff recognized that he could double the quantity of good clothing he owned if he was willing to sacrifice custom-made clothing. However, he found that wearing the best was worth the additional price to him.

Bud was willing to spend the extra money for top quality tools because experience had proven the extra cost well worth it.

How do you determine the quality you need? Many factors need to be considered. How long do you expect to use the product? What use do you anticipate? If you're purchasing a tool for home use, and your home is like ours, you're more likely to lose the tool than you are to wear it out. However, a craftsman who expects years of use from his tools needs to be concerned with quality.

How important is it to you to know that you have purchased the best quality? Just knowing that you have the very best may give you an attitude of confidence that makes you more effective in your relationship with others. Another important consideration is your perception of how others are affected by the quality of your purchase. Is it important to you that others be favorably impressed? This is a valid consideration in deciding what quality item you wish to purchase.

3. How should I pay for my purchase.

We'll discuss the use of credit later on, but the basic rule to follow is this: If you can't afford to pay cash, you can't afford to make the purchase.

4. Where to shop?

a. First, remember that you pay for brand names. Advertising, in order to establish a brand name identity with the buying public, costs a great deal of money. This cost is added to the price of the product.

Because of this money, the brand identification becomes a valuable commodity to the owner. Companies go to great lengths to protect their brand names. Simultaneously, these same companies are subject to over-production, changes of styles, and other factors that may cause over-production.

Sy Syms has developed a thriving business by selling name brand merchandise at substantial discounts. The only difference between Sy's merchandise and that carried by major department stores is that the name brand label has been removed from clothing. Generic foods currently carried in many supermarkets sell at substantial discounts even though they are being produced by manufacurers who produce the name brand items.

Check the area in which you live for off-price merchants such as Sy Syms. Taste-test generic grocery items to see if their quality is sufficient·to meet your standards.

b. Secondly, can you cut out the middle man? Middle men perform an important function in our system of merchandising, but their services and distribution cost money. Anytime you can purchase from a factory outlet or directly from a wholesaler, you are likely to save money. Sam Furrow made his Pay-Less Cashways stores among the most profitable ·home centers in the country partly by eliminating the middle man. The same principles that made Sam Furrow's stores prosper can save you money.

Another factor to consider is the volume of merchandise the store moves. A normal rule of thumb is that the higher the volume the better the price. This is often the reason discount merchandisers are able to offer attractive prices.

In addition to discount houses, it would be wise to check the prices through catalogue purchases. Catalogues can often be particularly helpful when shopping for specialty items that are unlikely to be sold in volume no matter what the population of your locality.

5. Whenever possible, shop by phone. Many people with good shopping discipline lose everything they might have saved by trudging from store to store, without first learning which stores carry what they're interested in. Unless shopping is a recreation activity for you, (and it can be a valid recreation), use the phone to pinpoint the stores who have what you're looking for.

Shopping with Credit

Basic rule: If you don't have the cash, don't make the purchase. Credit cards and charge accounts should only be used when you have the money in the bank to pay them off, and when there is no interest charged for using the credit.

Don is a 27-year-old C.P.A. with an accounting firm. He travels extensively and always charges his travel expenses on one or another of his credit cards. "Just look at the money I'm making," he says. "On many months I have $5,000 in charges on which I'm paying no interest. Think of the interest I'm earning on that money."

A closer examination reveals a different situation. On those charge accounts which allow extended payments, Don has used his credit limit while making only minimum payments. When asked what he did with the reimbursement checks for those travel expenses, he admitted that he found it easy to spend them on other items. When the credit card bills come due, Don finds himself scrambling to find the funds to pay them, even though he has already been reimbursed for the expenses. Don's situation is a common one. He began using credit cards with the good intention of using other peoples' money, but finds instead that he has used the funds merely to expand his lifestyle.

Few of us are disciplined enough to use credit cards without going into debt. If you are just beginning to develop shopping discipline, get rid of all the credit cards. You'll be amazed at the number of businesses who will accept cash.

Shopping for Services

People who are otherwise careful shoppers often forget to include services such as medical, legal, accounting, or even home repair on their shopping list. The amount of money involved in these items can often be quite large, and they should be considered when you plan your shopping.

There are several reasons for the hesitancy to shop for these services. One is that most of us are quite ignorant about just what we're purchasing. Another is that often the personal relationship with the professional is at least as important to us as the service itself. Don't be afraid to ask a doctor or dentist what he charges for a given service. Prices in health care vary greatly. Check the cost of the different hospitals in your area and tell your doctor which hospital you prefer to be in.

Don't be afraid to check on legal or accounting costs. A local C.P.A. is likely to have significantly lower charges than a nationwide firm with offices in your city. If you need personal accounting services, the local accountant is likely to give as good, or better, service than the larger firm. Also, not all accounting needs require the services of a C.P.A. Non-certified public accountants may be able to satisfy your personal accounting needs at a much more reasonable price than a certified public accountant.

Don't be afraid to check with our attorney on the cost of services provided. Don't be upset if your attorney refers you to a junior partner in the firm to perform rather routine legal tasks such as the making up of a will. (Of course, if your estate is of any size at all, you will probably want to utilize the attorney who specializes in estate planning. No sense saving a few dollars now to the detriment of your family later.) A successful attorney's time is quite valuable. A senior firm member owes it to the other partners in the firm to use his time in such a way as to maximize the firm's income. He may be doing you a favor in minimizing your cost by utilizing the less expensive services of a junior partner, while still overseeing the quality of your legal needs.

Don't expect to get something for nothing. Your doctor, dentist, or attorney earn their living by providing knowledge for a fee. Don't attempt to get legal or medical advice in a social setting without providing remuneration. Taking a product without paying for it is stealing, whether the product is something material—or knowledge.

Buying a Car

Dale is a 37-year-old surgeon living in Minneapolis. He and his wife, Mona, have two cars. Mona drives a three-year-old station wagon which they own, to perform such tasks as grocery shopping, taking the children to music classes and sporting events, and a hundred other mother's chores.

Dale drives a new Jaguar sedan that he leases through his medical practice. "I always lease my car," Dale says. "I can change cars as often as I want. It's easy to keep track of the expenses as a business deduction. And, best of all, I don't have my money tied up; it's actually cheaper than buying a car."

Dale is right about the convenience of changing cars as often as he likes and the ease of accounting for a business deduction. But he is wrong about saving money. He is actually paying for the convenience of his frequent changes in automobiles and the ease of accounting. The only time to lease a car is if you recognize that you're paying a premium for the convenience.

A car is one of those items I believe should be purchased for cash. If you're buying a car for transportation, buy one that you can afford. If you don't have the money to pay cash for the car you want, buy an inexpensive used car and save the money you would otherwise use for making payments.

107

Your best value will always be a used car. Merely driving a new car around the block depreciates its value by 20% or more.

If you decide to purchase a new automobile, here are a few suggestions to help get the most from your money. Once you've selected make and model, shop several dealers for price. Never trade in your own car for a discount on the purchase of a new automobile. Merely handling your car increases costs for the dealer, and he must necessarily cover those costs either by increasing the price of your new car or decreasing the purchase price of your old one.

When ordering a new car, watch out for extra equipment charges. If you don't need it, don't order it. Extra equipment can double the price of a car.

Once you determine that the dealer has offered his best price, make him an offer at less than his quote with the cash in hand. You'll be amazed at the impact of that "green stuff" on prices. Never finance longer than you have to; always pay cash for an automobile when possible. If you must finance the car, arrange for your own financing and insurance.

Purchase extended service agreements on a car only if you're dealing with a new or untested model. If you're buying a car with a proven record and low maintenance costs, chances are that the cost of the service agreement would not be worthwhile.

There are two timing situations that might give you an advantage in the price you pay for your car. First, always check the price or make your cash offer toward the end of the month. If business has been better than normal, the dealer may already have covered his overhead and may be willing to take less profit. If business has been poor, the dealer may feel pressure to move the car even though it means taking less profit than he would like.

Secondly, check prices during or toward the end of an extended period of bad weather. If weather has kept people out of the showroom for a time, it may have created a situation where the dealer is willing to take whatever he can get in order to move the car.

In most cases, the purchase of another vehicle entails not only the purchase itself, but also the sale of your old car. Be sure you dispose of the car yourself. Advertising the automobile for sale in the classified section of the newspaper normally brings a quick response. Your banker will be happy to give you the "Blue Book" price quote for your car so that you have some idea of how to price it.

Also, a few dollars spent in touching up the paint or body work, giving your car a good wax job or other cosmetic work as needed, will normally increase the value of the car many times the cost of sprucing it up.

Home Sweet Home

The biggest purchase most of us will ever make is for our home. In some cases, a home purchase turns out to be a good investment, but that shouldn't be the major reason for the purchase.

A home is shelter, a place of refuge. Your home should be a place that is the most attractive you can afford. The tax advantages and the ability to control housing costs make purchasing a home advantageous to most people.

There are suggestions that may help you increase the purchasing power of your home-buying dollar. If you know the general area of town in which you wish to live, you can save money by buying directly from the owner.

A broker provides a service in bringing the buyer and seller together. Obviously, he or she must be paid for this service. The normal charge for the broker's fee is 6% of the selling price, and, while the seller pays this fee, it normally adds to the asking price of the home. Recent court rulings have required broker fees to be negotiated, but even so, you can theoretically get a better price if you can deal directly with the owner.

I said, theoretically. In practice, if you have the right broker, he or she can save you enormous amounts of money. If you make your wishes very clear to the broker, he or she can handle negotiations in an impersonal fashion, without provoking resentment. At this stage in my life, while conducting big money land deals, my broker is my right hand man.

For some, the disadvantages of yard maintenance, land cost, or other factors may entice them to purchase a condominium, cooperative apartment, or other such hybrid home. Consider the impact the costs beyond your control in such a purchase. In most condominiums and similar ownership arrangements, the owners' association will vote to determine the assessment for maintenance of common facilities. If you are going to be on a fixed income, locate a housing facility where the other tenants are likely to be in similar financial circumstances. That way, your interest in limiting costs will coincide with that of other tenants.

Buy your home because it is the place where you want to ·live. Investment consideration should be secondary. However, you're most likely to make a good investment in a home if you buy a place you like.

Remember!
- Teach yourself to be a disciplined shopper.
- Plan your shopping with a list.

- Whenever possible, cut out the middle man.
- Buy quality products only when you have a reason to believe they are worth the extra cost.
- Use the telephone to save shopping time.
- Shop for health, legal, accounting and other personal services.
- *PAY CASH!* If you can't afford to pay cash, you can't afford the product!

Chapter Eight

INVESTMENTS

The difference between investments and savings is a difference of purpose. Savings provide a short term objective, such as putting aside sufficient money to meet living expenses for three months, or saving for a vacation or a specific purchase.

Investing, on the other hand, is the placement of money with an eye to increasing your own net worth, for future retirement income or some other such objective. There are various vehicles for investing to meet your long-term objectives. The type of investment you choose depends on your objectives *AND* your personal psychological makeup.

Objectives include growth of funds, income from the investments, or security. While few of us have an objective that totally excludes the other two, you do need to evaluate what importance each of the three objectives plays in your future plans.

It is also important for you to evaluate your own investment psychology. If you are inclined to worry about your investments, finding it necessary to check every day for the slightest change in a stock investment or continually worrying about interest rate changes on a real estate investment, your investment should be very low risk. Obviously, such a low risk investment bears a lower rate of return. But there is no investment worth risking your peace of mind.

If, on the other hand, you're comfortable with a high-risk investment and find that fluctuations don't disturb you, your rate of return is likely to be higher.

Invest in Yourself

Ewing Kauffman is the founder and principal stockholder of Marion Laboratories in Kansas City, Missouri, and now a multi-millionaire. His many investments include ownership of the Kansas City Royals, but Kauffman considers the dollars plowed back into himself when founding Marion Laboratories his best investment.

For several years, Kauffman had been a pharmaceutical salesman in the Kansas City area. In those days, all the major laboratories supplied drugs in containers of 500 to 1,000 each. Kauffman saw the possibilities of providing medication in containers of 100 tablets, thereby making it unnecessary for the druggist to count tablets when filling the prescription.

Kauffman and his wife, with a couple of friends, began in the basement of the Kauffman home, buying drugs in large containers and transferring them to bottles of 100 tablets each. It was the beginning of Marion Labs, with the funds generated by the small surcharge on the smaller packages being reinvested until it made Mr. Kauffman one of the wealthiest men in America.

On a recent trip to Milwaukee, I chatted with a young black woman, obviously well-educated, who was driving the taxi from the airport to my hotel. As we continued our discussion, I learned she had a degree as a paralegal, but had found she could make more money driving a cab. She owned the taxi in which we were riding, as well as three others for which she had hired drivers. She mentioned that she had been able to save considerably from her profits and sought my advice on investing her money.

"Are you operating all the taxis you can efficiently operate?" I asked.

"No," she replied. "I think I could still make money with several more taxis."

"Then invest the money in the thing which has made money for you," I told her. "You should make outside investments only when you have reached the point of diminishing returns investing in yourself."

That's a difficult lesson for us to learn. We think in terms of investing, meaning that we have to give our money to someone else, but the best investment you can ever make is in yourself. Only when you have reached the point where you can no longer profitably invest in your own vehicle (job or company) should you seek to invest in others.

Recently, Fortune Magazine reviewed the personal wealth accrued to founders of 11 companies with public stock offerings in the first quarter of 1983. Each of the individuals had invested in themselves. It had paid off handsomely. The lowest net wealth shown was for $8.5 million, and the highest was Phillip Hwang, whose personal net worth was valued at over $794 million.

Mr. Hwang was a poor Korean immigrant when he arrived in the United States in the 1960's. He founded his company, Televideo, in 1976. The net worth from his company ownership alone is estimated at $769 million. Not a bad return for a seven-year investment in oneself.

Walk, Then Run

John is a 37-year-old insurance executive with a large firm headquartered in San Francisco. John joined the company soon after completing his M.B.A. at Stanford University, and quickly advanced, becoming a senior vice-president after only five years with the company. Talking with John about his job and his plans for the future, an all-too-common phenomenon emerges.

"I have a good job, but it'll be my investments which will make me rich," John relates. "I have a regular investment program and some day I'm going to hit it big."

When questioned about his investment decisions, John admits that he puts most of his money into highly-speculative stock issues, hoping to catch a "real winner." John admits that his record to date is not very good. Over the past three years, he has lost an average of $3,000 per year on his investments. But that doesn't discourage him. "I'm just paying my dues," he says.

The chances of John's ever becoming wealthy are very slim. Like many of us, he wants to start out rich. He wants to run before he learns to walk. Not only has this young executive lost money on his speculative investments, but the two or three hours a day of his company's time that he spends on the phone with his broker while reviewing new stock issues has caused a decrease in his productivity. The very thing that has provided him the money to invest, his high-paying job, is what he is now neglecting. And his supervisors are aware of it.

The First Step

How does one get started investing? Consider the following five-step plan for beginning your investment

116

program.

1. If the payments on your outstanding bills, loans, charge cards, etc., exceed 15% of your income, concentrate on reducing your indebtedness to the point where all these payments are less than 15%.

2. Set aside 5 to 15% per month of your income for savings.

3. Develop a "nest egg" equal to three months' income. You will invest this fund, but it should be invested in highly-liquid, very secure funds, such as a money market fund, short term certificate of deposit, or other investment that you can quickly convert to cash.

4. Develop an investment plan that emphasizes your goal, not how much you think you can put aside. The place to start with your investments is where you want to be, and then develop a program for arriving at your destination.

5. Diversify your investments. The old adage, "Don't put all your eggs in one basket," is particularly apt when referring to investments.

How to Double Your Money Every Five Years

Let's consider options. This is not intended to be a comprehensive listing of investment possibilities, but a review of capabilities open to you. Our overall goal in an investment program is to secure a return of 20%, thus doubling your money every five years. That may sound high to you, but studies of various investments over the past 15 years indicate that this is a reasonable rate of return with properly-selected high quality investment vehicles.

Investing in Stocks

Dozens of images come to mind when we think of stocks. Big corporations with skyscraper headquarters. Wall Street with its bustling crowds and noisy traffic. The New York Stock Exchange with men yelling at each other in a most uncivilized manner while exchanging millions of dollars per minute.

But just what is a stock? A stock is a certificate representing a percentage of ownership in a company and stated as a number of shares. The percentage of ownership obviously depends upon the number of shares outstanding. Ten shares in a company with only 100 shares outstanding represents 10% ownership. At the same time, 10 shares in a company with 1,000 shares represents only 1%.

There isn't sufficient space in this book to discuss all of the implications of stock investment. (For an excellent book on all aspects of investment, I recommend Venita Van Caspel's The Power of Money Dynamics.) But there are a few rules that you should consider when investing in stocks.

Allen Paulson is president, chairman of the board, and chief executive officer of the Gulf Stream Aerospace Corporation in Savannah, Georgia. The 61-year-old Paulson left home at the age of 13, holding odd jobs to support himself while attending high school. In 1951, after learning airplane mechanics as a 30-cent-per-hour trainee with TWA, Paulson founded a company to convert passenger aircraft into cargo planes. By 1978, with hard work and good management, Paulson had built his company to the point where his ownership made him a relatively wealthy man, certainly a millionaire.

But this wasn't enough for Allen Paulson. In 1978, mortgaging everything he owned and borrowing as much as he dared, Paulson purchased the Gulf Stream division of Grumman Aviation. People said he was crazy. That division had lost $2 million the year before. Corporate aircraft sales were in a slump. But, by April of 1983, Paulson offered stock in Gulf Stream Aerospace to the public and suddenly found his stock holdings worth over a half billion dollars. Not a bad investment.

Investment Rule #1: The best stock investment you can make is in a company in which you are in a position to influence the success of that company. Obviously, what we are talking about here is another form of investing in yourself. The people who make the most money on stock investment are those who invest in themselves.

Investment Rule #2: Always take advantage of someone else's willingness to pay for part of your stocks. Sounds obvious, doesn't it? However, do you know whether or not your company offers an employee stock purchase program? Many companies offer employees the opportunity of purchasing company stock with the organization itself paying part of the purchase price, or selling stock to the employee at a discount.

Investment Rule #3: Look for companies which have a high percentage of employee investment in the company.

Peoples Airlines is a low-cost, no-frill operation based in Newark, New Jersey International Airport. All employees of Peoples are required to purchase stock in the company. It's been a good investment for them. Many of the original employees are now millionaires because of their stock investments. Because of the interest of the employees/stockholders, the company has been profitable almost from the moment it started.

119

These hard-working, highly-motivated employees have made many outside investors quite a bit of money, also.

Investment Rule #4: Always try to select the dominant or leading company in a growth industry. The growth potential of industries change. In the early part of the 20th century, steel manufacturing, automobiles and railroads were the great growth industries of the United States.

Times do change. High technology companies, such as IBM, General Electric, and AT&T, tend to be the growth industries of the future. Service industries such as restaurant chains, temporary help services, and waste disposal companies have a high growth potential. It's important to remember that growth industries are not static—they change.

And that brings us to Rule #5—the most important rule of all. When investing in stock, it's essential that you watch your investments. Buying stock and hiding it away in a drawer is not only likely to fail to make you rich, it could very well help you end up in the poorhouse. Companies are dynamic. Industries change. Selecting your individual stock investment requires a great deal of study and constant supervision.

But what can a person do who doesn't have the time to supervise his own stock investment? That's simple. Hire it done. But you say, "I don't have the $100,000 minimum investment that's normally required to hire a financial manager." That's the beauty of mutual funds. When buying shares of a mutual fund, what you are doing is investing in an investment company. The stock portfolio of a mutual fund is selected by full-time professional managers. The objectives of different mutual funds vary—some are set up for growth, others for continuous income—but once stated must be pursued unless a change is approved by the mutual fund shareholders. If you don't have time to select and manage your own stock portfolio, utilizing the services of the professional managers of a mutual fund may be the answer for you.

Review the past performance of the fund. Many mutual funds have achieved outstanding growth performance, with several of them returning more than 20% per year over the past ten years. A carefully selected mutual fund can be an excellent investment.

Whether you invest in stocks of your own choosing or utilize the professional management of a mutual fund, remember that stock prices can go down as well as up. There is no guarantee of income or return of capital. With sound judgment based on past performance and a careful estimation of the future potential, stocks and/or mutual funds can be a profitable investment for you.

Real Estate Investments

In the autumn of 1982, Forbes Magazine published an article on the four hundred richest people in America. Of those who were first generation millionaires, starting with nothing and making money themselves, the most frequent source of that wealth was in real estate. There is money to be made in real estate—a great deal of money—but that money is not sure fire.

Those who make money in real estate appear to have two characteristics in common: 1) they purchase the real estate for an income-producing purpose rather than just an investment. 2) the investors have staying power. By staying power, I mean that because of income produced by the property itself, the successful real estate investor is never in the position of having to sell his property. Successful real estate investing is similar to successful stock investing. Real estate investments must be carefully selected and continually supervised. This is particularly true with rental property. It takes a lot of time and careful attention to successfully manage rental properties, though the rewards can be great. Just as mutual funds give one the option of professional management in stock investments, so real estate limited partnerships and syndicates can provide professional management for the real estate investor who does not have time to supervise his investments.

Selection of the real estate syndication of partnership should be based on three factors. The most important is the track record, or history, of the management team or general partner. The second factor to consider is the amount of leverage to be used—that is, the amount of borrowed funds compared to capital raised for the investment. The higher the percentage of borrowed funds, the greater the possible return, but also the greater the risk involved, especially during times of high or fluctuating interest rates. The third factor is the individual or firm offering the syndication for sale. A registered syndication offered for sale by a member of the New York Stock Exchange or other registered security dealer is much more likely to be a successful investment than an unregistered offering presented by a high-pressure sales outfit.

Careful selection and good management can make real estate a sound investment.

There's Still Money in Black Gold

Some of the greatest fortunes of the world have been made through the discovery, production, marketing, and servicing of oil and its production. The fabulous wealth of the Hunts and the Rockefellers, the fortune of the legendary Howard Hughes, and the incredible riches of Middle Eastern rulers all have been based on oil.

While the opportunities for a wildcat discovery making overnight millionaires have greatly diminished from a few years ago, the oil industry has matured to produce solid opportunities for low-risk, high-return investments.

Any time the production cost of oil is less than half the market price, oil syndicates are an excellent investment. As an example, current costs of purchasing known reserves in the ground amount to between $3.50 and $7.00 per barrel. Production costs have held steady and, in some cases, actually declined. Often $5.00 per barrel is the maximum charge for bringing the oil to the surface. With a market price of $30.00 a barrel, it should come as no surprise that oil production can be quite attractive.

There are two basic types of oil syndication investments. One is an income fund, where the management purchases proven oil reserves and then brings the oil into production. The other type of oil investment syndication is for exploratory purposes. Exploratory syndications range all the way from drilling in areas with currently-producing wells, to highly-speculative drillings in areas where oil reserves have never been proven.

Apply the same rules to selecting an oil syndication investment that you would apply to a real estate syndication. That is, evaluate the track record of the management, analyze the leverage being used, and be sure the firm is one you can trust.

A Note on Other Investments

Obviously, there are many other investments to be made besides stocks, real estate and oil. A few notes may be helpful.

Investing in commodities: whether it be gold, grain, or stock futures, the secret to successful commodity investing is to find a good trader with a proven track record. Then take his advice. Many people initially make money on the advice of a good trader, then allow their ego to get in the way. They wander off on their own and fail to take the advice that made them money in the first place. Commodity investment is highly speculative. Don't risk any more than you can afford to lose.

On collectibles: collectibles are likely to prove good investments only in times of high inflation. The most successful investors in collectibles that I have known actually made money by mistake. They started purchasing items they liked, only to find that those turned out to be good investments later.

Municipal bonds: only those in a very high income tax bracket will find the return from municipal bonds, because of their exemption from federal income tax, to be attractive.

One More Time

The most important investment you can make is in yourself. You are most likely to achieve your goals toward monetary security by finding something that you like to do, and then doing it as well as you possibly can. Don't mistake the difficulty you may have in getting started at a given task as an indicator that you don't like what you're doing. Even the most successful people have difficulty getting started at times.

I recently had the opportunity of spending time with

Bill and Janet Dailey. Janet is the best selling author alive. Her romantic novels have sold over 95 million copies! During our discussion, Janet mentioned that the role of her husband, Bill, a successful land developer, is not only to manage her earnings and to do the background research for her novels, but, most importantly, to force Janet to start and complete a minimum amount of writing each day. In spite of her enormous success, Janet said, "I still find it hard to start writing each day!"

The biggest mistake most people make is quitting a job or an occupation before they have spent enough time with it to really know whether or not it is something that can capture their imagination and their total energies. It is that kind of dedication to a task, whatever it might be, that is the best investment that an individual can possibly make.

Remember!

- Investing in yourself provides the highest return.
- Start your investment program by walking, then you can run.
- Retire debts until monthly payments are less than 15% of your income.
- Save regulary—5 to 15% of your income.
- Build a nest egg equal to three months income.
- Develop an investment plan.
- In any investment, evaluate the manager's past performance, the project leverage, and the person or firm selling the investment.
- Don't quit a job or project just because it's hard to get started.

- Give it a chance! Stick with a project, job or profession long enough to give time to capture your energy and imagination.
- Remember the five keys to success:
1. Dreams
2. Attitude
3. Work
4. Proper vehicle
5. Duplication

OTHER BOOKS
BY
DEXTER AND BIRDIE YAGER

Don't Let Anybody Steal Your Dream
Dexter Yager with Douglas Wead

This classic in the field of motivational writing has sold more than a million copies and is selling as well today as it did in 1978 when it was first published. Dexter Yager has influenced millions with his forthright honesty, compassion and desire to see others succeed. Here is a man who has "made it" in all the right ways, and who is willing to pour out the ideas that make for successful living.
Paperback: $4.95 Stock No. BK-10
Hardback: $6.95

Becoming Rich
Dexter Yager and Doug Wead

Inspirational and moving stories of some of the world's greatest people and the eleven principles behind their success. Includes Walt Disney, Albert Einstein, Martin Luther King, Andrew Carnegie, Adolph Ochs, Jackie Robinson, Thomas Edison, Helen Keller, Harry Truman, Coco Chanel, Winston Churchill, Arturo Toscanini, and Douglas MacArthur.
Paperback: $4.95 Stock No. BK-97

The Secret of Living is Giving
Birdie Yager with Gloria Wead

Birdie Yager, wife of one of America's most famous and powerful businessmen, talks about:
• Marriage: How to make it work.
• Attitude: The way to popularity and self-esteem.
• Your Husband: How to make him rich!
• Children: When to say no, and when to say yes.
• Health and Beauty: They are the result of decisions, and are not automatic.
• Money: When it is bad; when it can be wonderful.
• Faith in God: Why you must deal with your guilt and inferiority, or self-destruct.
Paperback: $3.95 Stock No. BK-96

127

Millionaire Mentality
Dexter Yager with Doug Wead

At last! A book on financial responsibility by one of America's financial wizards, Dexter Yager! Dexter gives freely of his remarkable business acumen, teaching you how to take inventory and plan for financial independence.

Here is a common sense, down-to-earth book about investments, shopping, credit and car buying, and budgeting time and money.

Included are anecdotes about other successful American business people—to give you ideas about where to go from here!

If you are serious about financial planning, this is the book for you!
Paperback: $4.95 Stock No. BK-206

The Business Handbook
Dexter Yager

The most comprehensive how-to-do-it manual ever offered!

A simple yet detailed guide that lets you chart your own path to success in Amway.

The Business Handbook brings you the best in proven techniques regardless of whether you want to earn just a little extra income or if you are interested in building a large successful organization.

Discover what MLM or Network Marketing (as revealed in Megatrends) really is and how it differs from Direct Marketing and Pyramiding.

Awaken yourself to the proven advantages offered through the Amway phenomenon.

Learn the importance of:
• Winning
• Leadership
• Goalsetting
• Loyalty
• Dreambuilding

Discover the secret techniques used by many successful distributors who have become millionaires and are fulfilling their greatest dreams.
Paperback: $6.95 Stock No. BK-247

Successful Family Ties:
Developing Right Relationships for Lasting Success.
Ron Ball with Dexter Yager

Right Relationships with the people around you are fundamental to your success in life—emotionally, spiritually, and even in your work. This book will give you high performance, practical guidelines for dealing with the many important issues that may be holding you back from experiencing success in your family relationships. You'll learn to recognize the signs of trouble and to take steps toward overcoming.
- ruptured relationships
- busy signals in communication
- sexual temptation
- stress
- selfishness
- negative people

And with principles founded on God-given, timeless truths you'll discover lasting success in all your challenges and be sure to have successful family ties.
Hardback: $10.95 Stock No. BK-310

A Millionaire Common Sense Approach to Wealth
Dexter Yager with Ron Ball

Finally! A book that brings the sometimes complicated and misunderstood concept of wealth to the level of understanding of the common man. In a common sense, straight forward way, this millionaire shares his sometimes bold and very candid approach to accumulating wealth.

With all his experience in business and life in general he is indisputably a wise man. And with this wisdom and honesty he talks about:
misconcepts about money and materialism, eleven reasons to be rich, the principles of: work, dreams, people, perseverance, and investment. He continues with information on breaking budget barriers, doing a personal financial analysis, developing a common sense about managing money, and the spiritual secret of true success.
Paperback: $6.95 Stock No. BK-315

The Mark of A Millionaire
Dexter Yager & Ron Ball

Dexter Yager's financial accomplishments are world-renowned. Now his life principles are revealed in plain terms.

There is no mystery to success. It is achieved by those who understand its reasons. Here is a book filled with proven methods that will make your success happen!

• How do you specify a life target?
• What is a success plan?
• How do you overcome killer stress as you climb higher?
• Why is your personal image so vital?
• What is the key spiritual dimension in material accomplishment?
• How do you keep your success once you've won it?

The answers are in the pages of this book.

The Mark of a Millionaire is like attending a private graduate course in real-life achievement given by a man who has not only done it but continues to do it everyday.

These principles work!

Paperback: $6.95 Stock No. BK-334

Available from your distributor, local bookstore, or write to:

Internet Services Corporation
P.O. Box 412080
Charlotte, NC 28241

Please include $5.00 for shipping and handling.